WALLACE LOCKHART has resided in his adopted town c
years, and has made a worthy contribution to life in
member and past president of both Linlithgow Ru
Country Dance Club. He served as chairman and treasurer of the old League of
Friends of St Michael's Hospital, is a former elder of St Michael's Parish Church,
and has been prominent for many years as leader of Quern, possibly the most
widely travelled amateur music group in Scotland. He scripted and produced the
musical presentation 'Linlithgow's Story', which, as well as having been presented locally in the House of the Binns, Cross House and St Michael's Kirk Hall, was
performed in French to audiences from twin town Guyancourt in the undercroft
of Linlithgow Palace.

Wallace serves as a guide to visitors to St Michael's Church and is involved
with Linlithgow Union Canal Society, the Ramblers and Hillwalkers and, as he says,
anyone he can share a tune with. He is especially proud of the fact that all his
family have elected to live in the town.

By the same author

On the Trail of Robert Service (Luath Press)
Highland Balls and Village Halls (Luath Press)
Fiddles and Folk (Luath Press)
The Scottish Wedding Book (Luath Press)
The Scots and Their Oats (Birlinn)
The Scots and Their Fish (Birlinn)

Linlithgow Life and Times

G W LOCKHART

Luath Press Limited

EDINBURGH

www.luath.co.uk

First Published 2006

ISBN (10): 1-905222-39-4
ISBN (13): 978-1-9-0522239-1

The paper used in this book is acid-free, neutral-sized and recyclable.
It is made from low chlorine pulps produced in a low energy, low
emission manner from renewable forests.

Printed and bound by
Thomson Litho, East Kilbride

Map by Jim Lewis

Typeset in 10.5 point Sabon

To all my family and friends in Linlithgow

Acknowledgements

This book would not have been possible without the help of a great number of people who, without complaint, indeed with a great deal of enthusiasm, fed me information, answered my questions, helped in research, read over my draft writings and generally made me feel I was doing something worthwhile. To all, I express my sincere thanks for their tolerance and help. In particular I acknowledge the following:

Rev. Ian Paterson – St Michael's Church

Historic Scotland staff at Linlithgow Palace

John Aitken & Colin Galloway – Linlithgow Union Canal Society

Ian Donaldson – Chairman, Linlithgow Twinning Association

Joy McIntyre – Linlithgow Link

Colin McGill – Chairman of Board, Laetare International Hostel

Bob Smith, for information on fishing on Linlithgow Loch

Jim MacIntyre & Malcolm Porteous, for information on the loch as a bird sanctuary

George Thomson – Outdoor Education Manager, Low Port Centre

Heather Knox – Linlithgow Scottish Country Dance Club

Julia Wade & Tony Smith – Linlithgow Civic Trust

Julia Wade, David Lunt & Ian Osborne – Linlithgow Arts Guild

The late Peter Sutherland – Countryside Manager, Beecraigs Country Park

Grace McClure – Linlithgow Folk Festival Association

George Strachan & Jim Wilson – West Lothian County Cricket Club

John Davidson – Founder and current secretary, Linlithgow Ramblers and Hill Walkers

Alan Young – Chairman, Linlithgow Heritage Trust

Hector Woodhouse – Former Provost of the Deacons Court

Leslie Donaldson & David Roy – Linlithgow Rose Football Club

Gerry Keating & Bert Lawson – Linlithgow Rugby Football Club

Marshall Green – Seeds of Hope

Judy & John Barker – Linlithgow Players

Ena Bennie & Stan Matassa – Linlithgow Golf Club

Eddie McKenna & Jo Laverty – Linlithgow Reed Band

Hector Woodhouse & Martin Fleming – Linlithgow Sports Club

Colin & Linda Stein, Alan Old – Linlithgow Bowling Club

Murdoch Kennedy & Forbes Kennedy, for help with 'Lithca Lore'; and Forbes Kennedy for permission to extract from 'The Missing Black Bitch'

Iris McGowran MBE, for help with 'Some Noteworthy Figures of the Town'

Fiona Scott & Margaret Brown, 'Linlithgow Amateur Musical Productions'

Evelyn Kidd, for help with 'Children's Gala Day'

Terri Taylor, for her wonderful photography

and old friend Harry Knox, for various bits and pieces.

Contents

Foreword

by Tam Dalyell

SOME MONTHS AGO Wallace Lockhart and his music group Quern came to the Binns to present, in aid of the National Trust, a musical journey entitled 'Linlithgow's Story'. It was a splendid evening as a full house, against a background of music associated with the town, listened to a well researched story of Linlithgow over two thousand years.

In his new book, Wallace looks at Linlithgow from a different angle. Certainly there is an amount of history to be read but the focus is on contemporary and recent-past life in the town. This is all to the good. Present life will become history in turn and should be recorded. And a wider population should be aware that beyond the palace and the traditions of which we are rightly proud, Linlithgow is today a vibrant community harbouring people from all over. This can be seen in the staggering number of clubs and organisations which serve the population, and the number of initiatives coming to the fore which aim to keep the spirit of the town alive.

I am pleased to see reference in the book to Pop Brown of the *Gazette*. I well remember him at the wheel of his venerable Alvis vintage motor car 'proceeding' – I think that is an accurate description of his driving – up and down the High Street between the Johnston Offices and his home in 'the Brig'. Wallace performs a service in reminding us of our worthy citizens.

I wish this book the success it richly deserves.

Tam Dalyell
October 2006

Introduction

The Kirkgate

SEVENTEEN MILES WEST of Edinburgh, perhaps three miles south of the River Forth, is sited a very special town. It is special to some because of its abundance of historical connections. It is the birthplace of Mary Queen of Scots, scene of the assassination of Regent Moray, host to both Prince Charles Edward Stuart and the Duke of Cumberland, site of the church where James IV supposedly saw a vision before making off for Flodden... the list seems almost endless.

However, there is much more to Linlithgow than its history, or traditions such as the Riding of the Marches. Linlithgow is easy to describe: it is a town with a soul. Why this should be is not so easy to explain; still, I have yet to find anyone who disagrees with me in this description. Linlithgow's population has risen sharply over the last thirty years, from 6,000 to 15,000, owing largely to arrivals from many different places. There is a vitality about the population; as a friend who hails from another part of the country put it to me, 'In my area people talk about doing things, in Linlithgow people start things and follow through.' The proof of this is in the incredible number of clubs and associations which the town boasts, and in the town's ability to integrate its people. On the wall of the Rugby Club is a board listing the names of past presidents and club captains. The knowledgeable will tell you these men originate from both the Highlands and the Lowlands, from England, Ireland and Wales. And no one would ever suggest this list is unusual. It brings to life the town's motto that 'St Michael is Kind to Strangers', a statement that can be seen on the plinth marking St Michael's Well in the High Street.

This inclusiveness is not a new phenomenon. Alexander Smith, the pattern maker who became secretary of Edinburgh University, described his feelings about the town in his book *Dreamthorpe*, in somewhat idyllic terms:

> I first beheld Dreamthorpe, with its westward-looking windows painted by sunset, its children playing in the single straggling street, the mothers knitting at the open doors, the fathers standing about in long white blouses, chatting or smoking; the great tower of the ruined castle rising high into the rosy air, with a whole troop of swallows – skimming about its rents and fissures; – when I first beheld all of this, I felt instinctively that my knapsack might be taken off my shoulders, and that my tired feet might wander no more, that at last on the planet I had found a home.

In this book I have attempted to show something of the town's vigour. In order to set the scene I have inevitably had to resort to history in many cases. But my desire is to show how the old and the new are married; perhaps one of the simplest examples of this is the sight of 300 people dancing their summer Wednesday evenings away around the fountain in the palace courtyard. Linlithgow has given me much. I hope you, be you 'Black Bitch', incomer or visitor, will, like me, see it as a town of vigour, of honesty, of purpose, and, above all, as a town with a soul.

G W Lockhart
October 2006

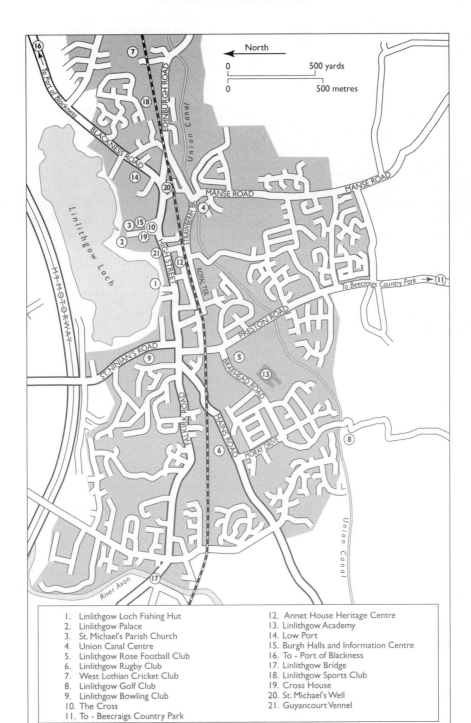

1. Linlithgow Loch Fishing Hut
2. Linlithgow Palace
3. St. Michael's Parish Church
4. Union Canal Centre
5. Linlithgow Rose Football Club
6. Linlithgow Rugby Club
7. West Lothian Cricket Club
8. Linlithgow Golf Club
9. Linlithgow Bowling Club
10. The Cross
11. To - Beecraigs Country Park
12. Annet House Heritage Centre
13. Linlithgow Academy
14. Low Port
15. Burgh Halls and Information Centre
16. To - Port of Blackness
17. Linlithgow Bridge
18. Linlithgow Sports Club
19. Cross House
20. St. Michael's Well
21. Guyancourt Vennel

CHAPTER I

Linlithgow Loch

Linlithgow Loch, a favourite spot for birdwatchers

LINLITHGOW WITHOUT ITS loch is unthinkable. To have the town in one's mind is to picture immediately the water of the loch with the palace and the Church of St Michael standing proud above it. How many have rushed home to grab their cameras and sought to capture that scene, especially when the sun dips in the sky exposing a silhouette at once romantic and compelling?

It is likely that the loch has given the town its name, which is considered to be more Brythonic-Celtic in origin than anything else. 'Lin' after all is a common expression in Scotland for water, although those from the north east with thoughts of Reekie Linn and the Linn of Dee to the fore will expect more froth and fury than Linlithgow Loch normally provides. The middle syllable 'lith' can be traced back to 'moist', while 'gow' is likely to have its roots in 'cau', or 'hollow.' The 'place by the lake in the moist hollow' is not a bad description of the town's location.

The loch today covers some 115 acres and is a healthy two miles round. It was not always this size and shape, however; adjoining lochs were once in existence and there was much surrounding marshland. We believe early inhabitants may have had to build their houses on stilts because of the high water table. Water drained from the surrounding slopes, and in prehistoric times the River Avon followed a different course and flowed through the valley occupied by the loch, continuing on to the headland where Blackness Castle now stands guard. Part of the loch in front of the palace was filled in in the nineteenth century. The little island opposite the palace is named 'the Rickle'. This is a particularly Scottish expression for a disorganised heap of just about anything, but it can also apply to a collection of small stones placed on larger ones. One wonders then if the island hosted a crannog at some period.

In view of what is to come, may I explain to any newcomer to Linlithgow that the name given to anyone born here is 'Black Bitch'. It is an honourable title which has absolutely nothing to do with race or gender, although it has from time to time caused consternation, such as when it has been used on the radio, and at least once when it came up in a parliamentary circle. A Black Bitch figures on the town's coat of arms. (I will not dwell on the Burns supper I once attended where some less than attentive printer caused pandemonium to reign by converting the Black Bitch on the menu cover to a Black Dog.)

Well, what has this got to do with Linlithgow Loch? Obviously the honoured title has an origin, and there is more than one suggestion as to what this could be. Some say it was merely a hunting dog, others that a black bitch roused the population when a fire broke out in the town. But let me relate my favourite legend, which is inspired by the loch:

In unspecified olden times the punishment for a crime such as murder was to be tied to a tree on an island in the loch and left to starve to death. Our story goes that one man had this punishment meted out to him but showed no signs of starving. Unable to understand this, a watch was kept and it was discovered that his dog, a black bitch, was swimming out to the island every night carrying sustenance to him. From this acorn-story an oak has grown.

It is interesting to note that reference to a black bitch is made in the Statistical Account of Linlithgow in the 1790s:

> no satisfactory account can be given how that animal came there, or should be so far dignified as to form a part of the town's armorial bearing.

Our conclusion is that the origins of the black bitch stretch further back into the past than is often suggested.

The loch appears on many postcards and prints. Let us go back to the long and hard winter of 1848, when the loch froze to such an extent that the cry so beloved of curlers went out: 'a Grand Match', the north against the south of Scotland, was to be held. Charles Lees painted the scene and, thanks to the Royal Caledonian Curling Club making his work available in print, has transported Linlithgow to houses throughout the world. Curling has always had a strong following in Linlithgow. Linlithgow Curling Club was founded in the 1700s and may well be the oldest Curling Club in Scotland – and that means in the world. Only one other club is in contention for the title; Kinross, beside Loch Leven. Both Linlithgow and Kinross have agreed to let the matter lie because, in each case, their original records have been lost.

Was anyone ever more enthusiastic about curling than baker Ebeneezer Oliphant, who reflected:

I like weel to hear o' the keen game o' curlin'
Though grey is my hair noo an' crazed are my banes,
For I mind sin', I cried like the Irishman's starlin'
'Will you let me oot wi' my besom and stanes?'

When auld John sat doun at the wast neuk o' Cockle
An' his banner displayed a' the lads wi' their brooms,
If the game was for fun or the medal was local
Oor teeth never chattered at auld Jocey Hume's.

We faught till the sun sank far south fae Ben Lomond,
An' slow was the slaughter for dour was the yoke,
An' wh'er the first star, strack its lamp 'the gloamin',
We campit a' nicht wi' a frien' at the Knock.

And for a taste of the bonspiel atmosphere on the loch one can do no better than a quote from an article by Graham Laurie:

The bad winter of 1963 meant outside curling; the loch froze enough to bear, and a match was organised for the weekend. The town at that time had many 'worthies' – not the least of them being Big Iain Mackay of the West Port Hotel, and my uncle John Laurie the butcher. Uncle John made a batch of haggis which we floated in hot water in a double-handed bath and which was carried, by myself and Peter Bain of the Red Lion down the garden, through the Peel, and over the ice to Craigie Brown's field (Fiddle's Croft), where the action was taking place. It was well received with great hilarity, then the bonspiel went on. And the whisky flowed.

The loch is a Mecca for those who like to spend their leisure hours out of doors. To quote Alexander Smith again in his essay *Dreamthorpe*:

> In summer I spend a good deal of time floating about the lake. The landing-place to which my boat is tethered is ruinous, like the chapel and palace, and my embarkation causes quite a stir in the sleepy little village. Small boys leave their games and mud pies and gather round in silence; they have seen me get off a hundred times, but their interest in the matter seems always new. Not unfrequently an idle cobbler, in red nightcap and leather apron, leans on a broken style, and honours my proceedings with his attention.

A closer look at loch life is warranted.

Fishing

Linlithgow Loch is one of Scotland's finest fisheries and some would rate it higher than that. Its ownership resides with Historic Scotland but for many years it has been leased to the Forth Area Federation of Anglers, which also has the care of lochs and lochans in Stirling and the Trossachs in its hands. The Federation is unusual in fishery management circles in that it is a non-profit making body. Volunteers carry out management decisions and do much of the other work too.

The loch's ability to hold and sustain so many fish of size is due to the prolific feeding grounds it possesses. It is shallow around the edges, but depths of 26 to 48 feet have been plumbed in the area in a line out from the palace. Fresh water shrimps, worms, snails, nymphs, flies and plankton all contribute to the loch's inhabitants' ability to put on weight. These inhabitants include brown and rainbow trout, pike and perch, eels, roach (sometimes known as 'braize' locally), stickleback and minnows. At one time efforts were made to run a brown trout hatchery using brought in eggs, but it was not a success, the small brownies released being quickly gobbled by pike. Today's policy is to stock weekly with rainbows, a policy that appears to be endorsed by local anglers. Permits for 12 rods to fish from the bank are available daily and two rods may fish from the nineteen fishery boats. Catch limits are set at four fish if fishing from the bank, six from a boat. The average size of fish caught is over the 2lb mark, but the loch contains many big fish and a few anglers have returned home with wide grins on their faces as they deposit a 13lb monster in the kitchen sink. The following table showing yearly catches will give an idea as to why a day on Linlithgow Loch is much sought after:

Year	Rods	Fish	Fish per rod
2001	4092	8664	2.11
2002	4050	8020	1.98
2003	3865	9440	2.44
2004	3896	8832	2.26

There is no doubt that the number of cormorants attacking fish in the loch is of considerable concern to fishermen. The decreasing fish stocks in the sea are resulting in less food being available for birds such as cormorants, and these birds are appearing in increasing numbers at fresh water fisheries. A 2lb trout is too big a mouthful for a cormorant no matter how hungry, but this won't stop the bird from trying, and the attempt results in a wounded fish.

A Congregation of Anglers

Fishermen are known for their tales, especially of the 'one that got away' variety, and Linlithgow has its share of these. Cruelly, it can be disclosed that some fishers have fallen from their boats into the loch, two hardies managed the almost impossible and capsized their boat, and more than a few have suffered both the loss of their outboard motor and the further indignity of having to row home. But there is one tale that must be told:

The fishing day is divided into sessions and fishers must prepare to return to the lodge when the warning hooter plays its tune. This is necessary so that fish can be weighed and boats cleaned for the next session. On this particular day a fishery official, in his own words, was spitting and swearing at a man and his wife who, 25 minutes after the hooter, showed no sign of making for the jetty. After a while he realised they were in some sort of trouble and was about to go to their aid when he saw they were at last heading homewards. Approaching land a large rusty anchor was seen hanging from their boat's bow, an Admiralty anchor of the kind issued to boats around a hundred feet long. This had been fouled by the fishing boat's grapnel and manhandled on board by the fisherman and his wife, who deserved plaudits for their strength. The onlookers had one question, how did such an anchor get into the loch? It was some time before the answer was found.

During the war, when the Wehrmacht were sweeping through Holland, Belgium and Northern France, they would land troops behind enemy lines on canals and lakes. As a counter to this, wire cables connected to tripods on rafts were slung across potentially vulnerable stretches of water – and Linlithgow Loch came into this category. The rafts were held in place by standard Admiralty anchors, one of which was now making a reappearance. It lies today behind the fishing lodge.

Sailing

Anyone walking round the loch on a winter Sunday 30 or 40 years ago would have been amazed at the sailing activity that was going on. For when winter conditions ruled out dinghy sailing on the Forth the answer was to make for Linlithgow Loch, and regattas were almost a weekly feature. The quality of sailing was high and nationally known racing figures could be recognised. The main users of the loch though were Edinburgh private schools, Edinburgh and Heriot-Watt Universities and Moray House College of Education.

Then, in 1974, with Frank Cooper as its first Commodore, Linlithgow Loch Sailing Club was formed. In the mid eighties the club was probably at its strongest, with a very active and competitive membership. Club members competed in regattas across Scotland and hosted many of their own for visiting sailors. Often, over 50 boats could be seen competing on the loch. It was at this time that a teenage Shirley Robertson received much of her early training, being coached by George Thomson, Outdoor Education Manager at the Low Port Centre and at that time coach to the national squad. Shirley would later make her mark by winning gold medals at the Sydney and Athens Olympic Games. Two brothers sailing at that time, also called Robertson but no relation to Shirley, would also make their mark by taking first and second in the World Enterprise Championships.

It was back in 1968, shortly after Linlithgow Academy moved from the Low Port to its current location, that West Lothian Youth and Community Service started the provision of an Outdoor Education programme on the site and began using the loch for canoeing and kayaking, and later for sailing and windsurfing as well. The programme was particularly designed to meet the needs of schools and youth groups. Progress over the years has been substantial and in 1997 the Low Port Centre was acknowledged as the National Centre of Excellence for Marathon and Sprint Canoeing.

A Linlithgow Kayak Racing Club has also been formed by local people, and Edinburgh and Heriot-Watt Universities continue to use the loch for sailing, often hosting competitive events for other universities.

Birdlife on the loch

Linlithgow Loch is rich in birdlife, as a walk round it will show. One cannot walk right round of course; there is a private area with restricted access abutting the east end of the park. This area is important as it contains a secluded and well sheltered bay offering birds protection from adverse weather.

The largest wildfowl on the loch are the swans and these are non-migratory. Mute swans are, as their name implies, generally silent, although they will hiss if annoyed. Their wings make a characteristic creaking sound when they fly. Adults have an entirely white plumage and an orange bill with a black nob. The male shares in the incubation of the eggs. Numbers have increased considerably in the last 30 years – largely due, it is thought, to excessive feeding by visitors – and sometimes over a hundred swans can be seen on the loch. Whooper swans, with their dark legs and yellow bill, are occasional winter visitors, but their visits are of short duration.

The loch is particularly important as a wintering refuge for several species of wildfowl, many of which migrate south from Northern Europe. While there is a year-round resident population of geese, winter brings the unmistakable Greylag, flying around in their distinctive 'V' formations, and a range of ducks including Mallard, Pochard, Tufted Duck and Goldeneye. The numbers of Mallards wintering have been falling in recent years, from a high of around 450 in the 1970s and 80s to nearer 150 at the present time. The Pochard population too has been drifting steadily downwards. In 1974 a winter count of 174 was obtained; by

2004 this had dropped to 105. Not difficult to recognise are the Great Crested Grebe and Little Grebe, who keep bobbing below the surface for food; Coots, Moorhens; and various gulls. The loch used to be one of the prime sites in Britain for the Great Crested Grebe, with considerable numbers breeding successfully in the reed beds at either end of the loch, but again numbers are declining. However, the Little Grebe or Dabchick is faring much better. Coots are popular birds with everyone. The white bony structure on the front of their skull gave rise to the expression 'as bald as a Coot.' They are fortunate in having, instead of webbed feet, webbed toes, thus allowing them to paddle in water and walk with ease on dry land. The Moorhen or Waterhen comes from the same family as the Coot, has a white splash under its tail and jerks its head as it swims.

As warmer weather is heralded, the bird population drops, with winter migrants returning to their northern haunts to breed. A number of birds will remain with us however, although that number appears to be dropping. An exception to this trend is the Mute swan. Its numbers have increased to such an extent that pairs now have a problem finding adequate breeding territories. Pairs of Mallards and Tufted Ducks attempt breeding each year with variable success. Coots and Moorhens manage much better.

There are a few rare visitors to the loch. One exotic American duck that has appeared in recent years is the Ruddy Duck. Those on Linlithgow Loch are feral birds descended from escapees from a wildfowl collection. Two particularly tame birds, probably also escapees, have attracted a lot of attention: a male Widgeon with a red head and yellow forehead has been associating with the tame Mallards, while a Red Crested Pochard with a 'bouffant hairstyle' has also been fraternising in the town bay. Less usual ducks which occasionally appear, either singly or in small numbers, include Gadwell, Teal, Pintail, Shoveller, Smew, Red Breasted Merganser and, devoid of a welcome from fishermen, the Goosander, with its ability to stay underwater for well over a minute. The Red-necked Grebe and Slavonian Grebe have also visited.

Perhaps surprisingly the very secretive Water Rail has been seen amongst the rushes near the small bridge at the west end of the loch. Occasional sightings include the brightly coloured Kingfisher and the motionless Heron.

Linlithgow Loch is one of the very few natural lochs in the Lothians and it is very much part of the town centre and open to people. The birds have become so accustomed to people and the people so accustomed to the birds it is easy to forget they are wild creatures that should be encouraged to forage for their food.

One sees frequently in North America, because of the population's fear of water pollution, stronger injunctions not to feed wild birds than we are accustomed to in Scotland. It is probably time we gave more attention to this serious matter before we are all the losers.

CHAPTER 2

Linlithgow Palace

Of all the palaces so fair,
Built for the royal dwelling,
In Scotland, far beyond compare
Linlithgow is excelling;
And in its park in jovial June,
How sweet the merry linnet's tune.

Sir Walter Scott

Linlithgow Palace, with the Crown of Thorns atop St Michael's Church (*left*)

IT IS IN July and August, rather than the June mentioned by Sir Walter Scott, that we nowadays look for joviality and music in the palace. For six Wednesday evenings during these months the palace courtyard is crammed with country dancers revelling, not just with the music, but in the unique atmosphere that prevails within these historic walls. It is doubtful if anywhere else in Scotland visitors to our shores have such ready access to Scottish music and dance in such romantic surroundings.

Not that music and dance are new to the palace; history has recorded many occasions of merriment. James IV in particular liked a party and is credited, or blamed, with the introduction of 'the Daft Days', when the court would travel to the palace to bring in the New Year in style. The original Daft Days were Yule, Hogmany, New Year's Day and Handsel Monday, the first Monday of the New Year, but James seemed to have had few qualms about extending the period. The poet James Ferguson was happy to describe the scene:

When merry Yule-day comes, I trow
You'll scantlins find a hungry mou';
Sma' are our cares, our stamacks fou
O' gusty gear,
And kickshaws, strangers to our view,
Sin Fairn-year.

Fiddlers, your pins in temper fix,
And roset weel your fiddle-sticks,
But banish vile Italian tricks
From out your quorum:
Nor fortes wi' pianos mix,
Gie's Tulloch Gorum.

It is thought the palace as we know it today originated as a royal hunting lodge or castle, and it was so used in the time of David I. The first description of the castle is dated 1301, when Edward I of England stayed there during one of his forays into Scotland. Later it was expanded and a peel, a defensive stockade or palisade, was built. The provision of a ditch on the town side of the hillock meant that, incorporating the water from the loch and marsh, today's church and palace area was at one time virtually an island. It is perhaps surprising that William Wallace, who was so active in the area before and after his battle at Falkirk, seems to have ignored the castle. The same cannot be said of Bruce. The castle was still in English hands in 1313. Here we encounter one of Linlithgow's great legends. Sir Walter Scott in his *Tales of a Grandfather* tells the story:

There was a strong castle near Lithgow, and there lived at no great distance from the stronghold, a farmer whose name was Binnock. This man saw the progress the Scots were making in recovering their country from the English, and resolved to help his countrymen by getting possession of the castle. Binnock supplied the garrison with cartloads of hay. The night before a delivery was due, he stationed a party of his friends near the entrance. Then he loaded a wagon with hay in which he placed eight well armed men. Binnock approached the castle early in the morning, and the watchman, seeing the expected cart, raised the portcullis. But as soon as the cart had got under the gateway, Binnock made a sign to his servant, who, with his axe cut the yoke which fastens the horses to the cart. At the same moment, Binnock, drawing his sword, killed the porter. The men then jumped from under the hay where they lay concealed and rushed on the English guard. The portcullis was let fall, but the grating was caught on the cart and so could not drop to the ground. The men who were in ambush near the gate ran to assist, and the castle was taken.

It is interesting that Sir Walter thought fit to abbreviate the town's name. Lithgow is the name of the town in Australia with which we in Linlithgow have some informal links, and where the town's music group, Quern, performed their musical presentation *Linlithgow's Story* in 1999.

Linithgow suffered a devastating fire in 1424 and St Michael's Church and the castle suffered along with the town's houses. James I came quickly to the rescue, and began rebuilding work. Apparently he decided he needed a comfortable palace more than an austere military base (although defences were by no means forgotten) and largely laid out the structure of what we can see today. To James IV we give the credit of modernising the palace to the sixteenth century style. Suites of royal apartments were positioned, the Great Hall received windows and a new roof, kitchens and ovens were liberally distributed. Then, sadly, we think of his Queen Margaret 'who in Lithgow's bower, All lonely sat and wept the weary hour', having to face the fact that her husband would not be returning from the bloody fields of Flodden.

Largely because he appointed a keeper with more than ordinary vision, the palace under James V is associated with elegance. Who has not admired the four orders of chivalry to which James belonged, positioned on the outer gate of the palace? (The Garter of England, the Thistle of Scotland, the Golden Fleece of Burgundy, and St Michael of France.) Who has not loved the magnificent fountain in the courtyard, which, in its day, was capable of flowing with either water or wine according to inclination? It is good the present caretakers have treated the fountain's maintenance so seriously. Specialist stonemasons have fitted a new cross and orb on its top and it has been restored to its former glory. No wonder when James' bride, Mary of Guise, arrived she thought she had never seen a more princely palace. But what did she think of the Riding of the Marches which we know took place in 1549, or the presentation in the palace of the great satire *The Three Estates* by Sir David Lyndsay?

The visit of Charles I resulted in a real spring cleaning, no less than 12 shillings being spent on dusters for 'dichting doune the haill mouse webbis (spiders' webs)

The Restored Fountain in the Palace Courtyard

throw the haill palace'. Later Cromwell was to enjoy its comforts while his troops ensconced themselves on the Peel. But it is the eighteenth century that really interests us. Prince Charles Edward Stuart spent a night in the palace in 1745. The next year it was the turn of the Duke of Cumberland. After his troops had left it was seen that the palace was burning. Whether by design or default we know not, since that time the palace has been unroofed and uninhabited.

So, what part does the palace play in Linlithgow life today?

First, let us look at the Peel. Although we now use the word Peel to describe all the parkland that surrounds the palace, originally the word was used to indicate its palisade or defensive limits. Fruit trees were once prominent in the Peel on ground terraced down to the loch. Bees were kept and, on the flat ground to the north of the palace, archery was practiced. Near that flat strip today sailing dinghies are parked, and a children's paddling pool is positioned at the east end. Round the loch walkers make much use of the Peel as do the runners in the various races held for the young and not so young. With its stunning palace background it has become a natural site for the staging of historical events, especially where battle scenes and jousting are involved. At a more sedate level, Historic Scotland Rangers offer children the opportunity to play nature detective and pursue such interests as 'minibeast hunts', 'loch dipping' and 'butterfly life'.

But the palace today is inextricably linked with tourism, with many thousands of visitors from all over the world arriving at the commanding ruin which has achieved fame as the birthplace of Mary Queen of Scots. We do well to focus on the courtyard of the palace and its fountain. At one time grass and cobbles made it less than appealing, but with a visit from the Queen in the offing in 1989, to celebrate the town's 600th anniversary as a Royal Burgh, someone somewhere in authority made the decision that the courtyard should be paved. To that anonymous person some thousands of visitors and dancers have expressed their thanks.

It was John Carsewell of the Country Dance Club who saw the potential for dancing offered by the paved courtyard. True, some dancing had taken place on the odd occasion in the somewhat exposed and draughty Great Hall of the palace, but the courtyard offered a special ambience. What particular problems John had to overcome before his dream became reality is not known, but in the summer of 1990 under the banner of 'Scottish Dancing for All', dancing took place on three Wednesday nights. 'Wednesdays in August' was the slogan that introduced the next year's series, when some clog dancers provided a cabaret of sorts. Expansion and improvements then took place, the town's Pipe Band adding colour to the scene and Walkers shortbread fortifying the dancers at the interval. Numbers were now passing the two hundred mark and, shortly after the rebranding of the dancing as 'Linlithgow Scotch Hop', the four hundred mark was reached. What makes a night at the Scotch Hop so amazing is the number of overseas visitors (and they range from American bankers to members of the Bolshoi Ballet) who, whether they speak English or not, are able with visible enthusiasm to enter into the spirit of Scottish country dancing.

The cream of Scottish country dance bands turn up to play at Scotch Hops. Bearing in mind the conditions of cold which may prevail, which are not always the happiest for musicians and instruments, it must be accepted there is a special something that attracts such bands to the palace. Recognition too must be given to West Lothian Council Arts Department and Scottish Traditions of Dance Trust for their support.

For another tourist-inclined innovation thanks are due to William Hendrie, the well known writer and former headmaster of Linlithgow Primary School, who has a reputation for making history alive and relevant. Mr Hendrie had his senior pupils dress in appropriate sixteenth century costumes and act as junior palace guides for the benefit of visiting school children. This is an approach which has found much favour with palace visitors. The teachers of school groups visiting the palace have access to prepared workbooks.

A special tourist attraction has been the series of enactments performed by the Linlithgow Players within the palace precincts. In costumes well worthy of the description gorgeous, the Players have given visitors a full impression of a range of historic occasions. The Players are dealt with more fully in Chapter 6 of this book.

As weddings move from the traditional to the romantic, so the palace has become a desirable place for holding ceremonies or as a photographic backdrop for the participants. The undercroft, where at one time knights would wait before being summoned to the King's presence, has been given sensitive refurbishment and, with its vaulted ceiling and polished wooden floor, makes an attractive venue for weddings, receptions and other functions such as medieval banquets and musical presentations.

There is one final story about the palace which must be told. Many old buildings are supposed to have their ghosts and Linlithgow Palace is no exception. It is a personal decision as to whether such stories should be accepted or not. The following is offered on that basis:

In 1989, to celebrate the 600th anniversary of Linlithgow as a Royal Burgh, a quite marvellous son et lumière was held. It told the story of the town and was enacted by the Players and various other groups and individuals. It started in St Michael's Church, the audience later moving over to the courtyard of the palace. Towards the end of the presentation there came the scene depicting the burning of the palace by the Duke of Cumberland's men. For effect, coloured lights played on a slowly revolving ball mirror while dried ice gave off some illusion of smoke. On the last night of the eight performances, the presentation over, the audience drifted away while members of the cast and some other helpers started to tidy up. The electricity was switched off. Suddenly there was a cry from a female member of the cast and it was obvious she was pointing to the ball mirror. There, on the ball mirror, was seen, perhaps by fifteen people, a face. It was the face of a woman dressed as Mary Queen of Scots might have been dressed in her time. In the opinion of one male member of the cast who saw it, the face might have lingered for a full two minutes. Then it disappeared. The writer makes no comment other than that the friend who gave him the story, and who saw the face, is, in his opinion, a most stable and reliable person. The press, of course, reported the incident. While accepting, a dozen or so people had seen something and reporting their comments, their tone was sceptical.

CHAPTER 3

The Union Canal and the Linlithgow Union Canal Society

TRANQUIL, PLACID, SOPORIFIC, hypnotic; how many adjectives can we think of to describe the peacefulness of still water? And the passing of a boat does little to spoil the ambience. It seems only to prove that all is well with the world.

Linlithgow is blessed with many locations of character; the Cross, St Michael's Church, Hamilton Lands, to name but a few. But the picture postcard canal basin has a special allure; the red slated buildings, the ducklings fleeing a barge seeking a mooring, the artists working in a world of their own.

The Popular Canal Fun Day

Make no mistake, this idyllic setting is only ours today because of the almost unbelievable commitment of a few of our fellow citizens. There is a tale to tell.

A good starting place is the 1790s. A growing Edinburgh was ravenous for coal – it was not to become known as 'Auld Reekie' for nothing. But bad or non-existing roads inhibited cheap commercial access to the great coalfields of Lanarkshire. Supplies to the capital came by ship from Fife, and even from as far away as Newcastle, and such seaborne activity fell foul of a tax. We can imagine envious glances being cast to the west where, thanks to the building of the Monklands canal, Glasgow was enjoying a supply of cheap coal. Inevitably there were discussions about how to improve the Edinburgh situation. Initial thinking was that a canal should be built linking Edinburgh and Leith with Lanarkshire, but gradually this plan was modified as the benefits of bringing in other population centres were considered. Then the Napoleonic War removed canal building from the agenda and it was not until 1813, when coal prices were very high, that things began properly to stir. Hugh Baird, who had supervised the building of the Forth and Clyde canal, was now charged with presenting plans for an Edinburgh and Glasgow Union canal. The plan he was to present would come under heavy attack from Leith, but success at the end of the day was to be his.

A direct link between Edinburgh and the Lanarkshire coalfields was out. Instead, the new canal would run from Lothian Road in Edinburgh to Ratho and the high ground behind Linlithgow, to marry up with the Forth and Clyde canal at Falkirk. A major advantage of this proposal was that it offered a stretch of over 30 miles of canal without the need for a lock until Falkirk was reached. Baird was optimistic about a passenger-carrying trade offering greater speed and comfort than a stagecoach, and saw the canal carrying goods ranging from quarried stone to oatmeal into Edinburgh. There was a certain amount of opposition to the proposal, but the appropriate legislation was prepared and the Act was passed through the House of Lords in June 1817. It envisaged:

> a direct, easy, expeditious and cheap conveyance for corn, coal, lime, manure, wares and merchandise between the cities of Edinburgh and Glasgow, and to and from the adjacent towns and places.

Baird now became the engineer in charge and, showing himself a man of taste as well as intelligence, took up residence in due course at what was to become Canal House at the basin. The canal itself would be five feet deep and extend to 45 feet wide at the surface. Three great aqueducts were required to be built and work on the twelve-arch aqueduct over the Avon commenced in 1819. It stands proud and impressive today, a popular walk with Linlithgow folk. The canal was completed in four years and formally opened amid great excitement in 1822. With changeover horses being available from stables every eight miles, the journey from Glasgow to Edinburgh could be done in only eight hours. (The present museum and tearoom were originally stables for four horses and accommodation for coal depot workers). Eventually six boats a day would make the passenger journey, with other barges catering for shorter hauls. In fact, by 1836 some 136,000 passengers a year were making use of the canal. The fare from Edinburgh to Linlithgow was two shillings. An overnight service known as 'The Hoolet' was introduced, much favoured, it was said, by honeymooners.

Alexander Smith remarked that the canal was the only thing that connected Linlithgow with the world:

It stands high, and from it the undulating country may be seen stretching away into the grey of distance. Every now and then a horse comes staggering along the towpath, trailing a sleepy barge filled with merchandise. A quiet indolent life these bargemen lead in the summer days. One lies stretched at his length on the sun-heated plank, his comrade sits smoking in the little dog-hutch. Silently they come and go. The horse stops at the bridge house for a drink, and there I like to talk a little with the men. They serve instead of a newspaper, and retail, with great willingness, the news they have picked up from town to town. The water hardly invites one to bathe in it, and a delicate stomach might suspect the flavour of eels caught therein; yet, to my thinking, it is not the least destitute of beauty.

Linlithgow industry welcomed the water it could now draw from the canal, the distillery of course using it only for its industrial needs, its distilling water coming from the town's wells, although in later years Loch Lomond would become a useful source.

The Union canal probably had twenty years or so of good trading conditions, especially with coal and stone, but by the 1840s, as they say, the writing began to appear on the wall. Railways were making their impact nationally. There were hopes that the rail link established in 1840 between Glasgow and the Slamannan basin would form a profitable integrated route between east and west, with coal being transferred at the Slamannan basin from rail trucks to barges. But within two years there was a change of mind and the railway line was extended all the way to Edinburgh. The Canal Company was forced to reduce its prices to meet the competition, but its passenger trade was declining rapidly. Although the canal had its commercial supporters, from this point on the story is a sad one. In 1848, the Edinburgh and Glasgow Union Canal Company was taken over by the Edinburgh and Glasgow Railway Company – this was just the beginning of a series of takeovers. The falling revenue meant less money available for dredging and general maintenance, although the company battled on bravely. The route into Edinburgh was shortened, the Lothian Road terminal being moved to Fountainbridge to allow land in the capital to be sold, but commercial traffic on the Union canal ceased to run in 1933. From that point on the canal was used only by recreational rowers and boating enthusiasts, with the St Andrews Club claiming it had used the Union for over a hundred years. After the war, when rail and water transport were nationalised, there was increasing pressure to close the canal completely. A Committee of Inquiry applied the 'coup de grace' and the Union canal was formally closed in 1965, although it retained the status of Remainder Waterway because of its importance to the drainage of Central Scotland. Who at that time could have foreseen the phoenix that would arise from the canal's ashes?

The Canal Fun Day

There is a cussed streak to be found in human nature. A frequent refusal in certain people to accept what the majority consider to be the inevitable. And in Scotland there is a passion for causes, be they lost ones like the Darien Scheme or fulfilling ones like saving a hospital. We admire men and women who combine vision with action and who are willing, in today's parlance, to put their head on the block. Such people were to come to the fore as the Union canal's degeneration continued.

The movement to restore the Union canal was slow in starting. It was first necessary to get an agreement to stop infilling and other actions which would inhibit restoration. Fortunately, came the hour, came the man, in the shape of Melville Gray – at that time a Linlithgow town councillor, later to become a regional councillor and then chairman of the Scottish Inland Waterways Association. With support from the newly formed Civic Trust, local interest in bringing the canal back to life was engendered, and the spring of 1975 saw the birth of the Linlithgow Union Canal Society, with Melville Gray as its first chairman. Within a year it had more than a hundred members. A hard physical slog was now to begin.

At that time today's colourful canal basin was in a derelict condition, the water shared prominence with rubbish and weeds, the towpath was a pitted track and the rusting wrecks of two canal barges were in desperate need of removal. One of those barges – which lay sunk by St Magdalene's distillery with 'U66' painted on her prow – has become something of a legend. A forty foot long, horse drawn scow, her working life involved carrying coal on the canal. The Society bought her for £25. Her holes were patched, a horse was borrowed, and the following year she was carrying passengers under the name *St Magdalene*. Today she lies in the Maritime museum in Irvine. But the best loved boat to be seen tied up in the basin is probably the *Victoria*. She was bought in 1978. One wonders how many artists have tried to capture the allure that hangs around her. She has certainly earned her keep and provided much publicity.

Much publicity for the Society also came from the Drambuie Marathon, which was run from 1975 to 1990. This involved two-man teams in inflatables with outboards making their way from Glasgow to Edinburgh along the Forth and Clyde and Union canals. Crowds turned out to cheer the teams through the basin each year, and a Society team provided the winners in 1987. Fund raising at this time had to be taken seriously, with dances, talks, slide shows and wine and cheese evenings all making their contributions. And few would deny that one of the most important decisions taken was to create Scotland's first and only canal museum. Much physical and technical work was carried out by volunteers in converting stables at the Manse Road basin into the attractive display unit that was opened by the town's MP, Tam Dalyell in the June of 1977. Over the years the museum has become a focus for school children, who come to learn about the canal and its importance to our environment.

During these early years, the Society's boat trips were limited to the west because of a culvert and thus one of the most important and dramatic parts of the canal, the Avon aqueduct, could not be reached. A campaign was started to have the culvert removed but success took time, it not being until 1992 that a replacement bridge was built, finally allowing access to the aqueduct. Various other battles against threats to navigation had to be fought, particularly when the Edinburgh bypass was at the planning stage. One spin-off from the Society's success at this time was that it encouraged people living the length of the canal to take a greater interest in its environment, and local societies were formed in Winchburgh, Ratho and Broxburn.

Over the years the Society's story has been one of hard work and expansion. Properties at the basin, such as the museum and tearoom, were rented from British Waterways, who also built the new slipway. Re-roofing and pointing of walls, the decoration of a tearoom, painting and joinery represent only some of the work the volunteer members have been involved in. In Linlithgow Union Canal Society property, new toilets have come into being, the surface of the quay improved. All this is vital work to support what the public have come to expect on and off the canal; boats in an ambiance of tidiness and colour.

The cardboard boat race is the highlight of the Fun Day

The canal itself requires much looking after. Weed cutting is a difficult and ongoing job, as is the regular review of the condition of the banks. Dredging is an unglamorous occupation. Towpath upgrading, painting, the building of ramps for the disabled; it seems there is no end to the background work that must be done. These tasks are undertaken by British Waterways. As the season comes to a close there is concern about what will be found when boats are lifted from the water for inspection and maintenance. Engines too require overhaul. All this is expensive work for which the society must pay the bill. It is the army of volunteers that keeps the show on the road. Income from boat trips is vital. Fund raising is non stop and the list of financial initiatives approaches the incredible, ranging from ghost walks and jumble sales to mugs, hats and Christmas cards, on top of the standard dances and social functions. The annual Fun Day is now an institution in the town, the crowds regarding the cardboard boat race as the highlight of the afternoon. The entry rules are simple; stay afloat as long as you can in a boat made from cardboard, string and adhesive.

As far as the public is concerned, the Society offers many recreational activities, including trips along the canal, mainly to the west. The journey to the Avon aqueduct takes just under the hour and is a favourite for both those looking for a quiet sail and those who want a group outing – for which a meal can be provided. Some couples, showing commendable initiative, have hired the *St Magdalene* for their wedding. Figures for 2004 show that the *Victoria* carried over 2,000 passengers, the *St Magdalene* over 1,700, while over 1,400 were carried on private charters. These are impressive numbers. LUCS is the only three star visitor attraction on the Lowland canals. The Falkirk Wheel has opened up new opportunities. Special cruises to the Wheel offer a day's outing. But the Wheel has opened up the canal system in Scotland as nothing else could and the increasing number of boats passing through Linlithgow is obvious to all. Many of these boats make use of the Linlithgow Canal Centre's services. The museum and attractive tearoom are open at weekends from Easter to October, and daily in July and August through the season commencing in April. The tearoom is often used as a function and meeting suite by local organisations, and for art exhibitions.

March 2006 saw the death of Mel Gray the Society's Honorary Vice-President The recipient of tremendous affection from all who knew him, it is not too much to say that without his vision and determination the Union Canal would not be the provider of the pleasure it gives the townspeople today. It is good when such a man sees his ambitions realised.

The year also saw the Linlithgow Union Canal Society receive funds, substantially from the Lottery and West Lothian Council, for the erection in the basin area of a Heritage Education Centre. So far educational input has been largely restricted to primary children in the small museum. Expansion will allow for exhibitions and lectures to be offered for all ages. And with the closer links being established with Further Education establishments it is hoped the canal and the Heritage centre will be seen more as a resource in the future suitable for field and rural studies.

THE LINLITHGOW UNION CANAL SOCIETY FLEET

Victoria – 12 passengers – available for charter
St Magdalene – 40 passengers – available for charter
Leamington – 12 passengers – self drive day boat
Slateford – 10 passengers – light passenger boat powered by outboard
Alex Inglis work boat – available for commercial charter (10 tons capacity)
J B work boat – light commercial charter

CHAPTER 4

The Music of the Town – from Folk to Opera

The Unofficial Headquarters of the Folk Festival Society

The Roke and the Wee Pickle Tow

AS ANY BAND or orchestra leader will tell you, there are certain tunes that have an innate ability to demand an immediate and uplifting response from people as soon as they are heard. In the traditional music field such tunes as 'Caddam Woods', 'The Irish Washerwoman' and 'The Atholl Highlanders' come to mind. In this select group also comes 'The Roke [or Rock] and the Wee Pickle Tow', the town march of Linlithgow. Its playing in the town demands immediate response; clapping, feet tapping, incoherent yells and pseudo dances. It is an injection of pride and joy. And as awkward to sing as the words are, one is forever surprised at the number of people who have mastered the task.

The title of the tune refers to the old type of spinning wheel and prepared flax. Burns, looking for the human aspect behind the material, makes the point, in his 'Epistle to Lapraik', that, as important as the actual piece of equipment was, more important was the social aspect of what it encouraged. Being mobile, the roke could be carried in to a neighbour's house. So, instead of today's coffee mornings, the ladies of Burns' time had 'rockings':

On Fasteneen we had a rockin,
To ca' the crack and weave our stockin;
And there was muckle fun and jockin,
Ye need na doubt;
At length we had a hearty yoking,
At sang about.

There was aye sang, amang the rest,
Aboon them a' it pleased me best,
That some kind husband had addrest,
To some sweet wife;
It thirled the heart-strings through the breast,
A' to the life.

Emmerson, in his *Scotland through her Country Dances*, points out that when cottage spinning became a thing of the past, a social meeting in the house of a neighbour (in the south west) was still called a 'rock'. When one neighbour said to another – 'I'm coming over with my rock', he simply meant that he intended to visit for the evening. (This is referred to in the Statistical Account relating to Muirkirk).

H. Grey Graham, in his *Social Life of Scotland in the 18th Century*, commented on 'Rockings':

On moonlit nights they held their favourite meeting in barns or cottage, called 'Rockings', when young women brought their rocks and reel, or distaffs and spindles – where young men assembled, and to the accompaniment of the spinning of the wool or flax the song and merriment went round, till the company dispersed, and the girls went home escorted by their swains, who carried gallantly their rocks over corn-rigs and moor.

The tune of 'The Roke' is old and we shall probably never learn of its true origin. Doubtless it came down in the oral tradition but John Glen, in his *Early Scottish Memories*, mentions the tune's appearance in Playford's *Music Hand Maiden* of 1663, where it is called 'A Scottish March'. The new title seems to have made its first appearance in James Oswald's *Curious Collection of Scots Tunes* in 1740.

Back in the seventeenth century, when the publishing of a song was indeed an event of note, the words would have been individualistic and probably bawdy. David Herd in his *Ancient and Modern Scottish Songs*, published in 1776, gives an untitled song to the tune of 'The Roke':

I hae a green purse and a wee pickle gowd,
A bonny piece land, and a planting on't,
It flattens my flocks, and my barns it has flowed;
But the best thing of a's yet wanting on't:
To grace it and trace it, and gie me delight,
To bless me and kiss me, and comfort my fight,
With beauty by day, and kindness by night,
And nae mair my lane gang faunt'ring on't,

But the words to 'The Roke' that are sung today are generally attributed to Alexander Ross who, as Kurt Wittig points out in *The Scottish Tradition in Literature*, wrote 'Wooed and Married and a''. Ross, a schoolmaster, was certainly dancing mad, as his words tell us:

He dances best that dances fast,
And loups at ilka reesing o't,
And claps his hands frae 'hough to hough',
And furls about the feezings o't.

But, standing at his grave by the cold waters of Loch Lee above Glen Esk in Angus, one wonders how his words came to be linked to a Central Scotland town. Well, 'The Roke' has certainly got to do with the manufacturing of material, and, as is pointed out elsewhere in this book, Linlithgow had its share of weavers. But was that enough for its adoption as a town's march? There is one story that has come the writer's way that may explain the link, and it is passed on here with a smile and without further comment. The story, the legend, call it what you will, is that at one time there was a citizen of the town who enjoyed a bit of wenching. One day while paying his respects to a lady, she gave out the cry 'Hide quick, my husband cometh.' In a house of little furniture, it was time for initiative. Seating the lady at her roke, he hid himself under her long gown and thus escaped detection. When the story of the incident got out, people would whistle 'The Roke' as they passed the unfortunate lover in the street. Another suggestion is that the tune is associated with the departure of James IV for Flodden.

The words used below are from David Herd's *Heroic Ballads* of 1776. It is recognised that other versions are now in use:

THE ROKE AND THE WEE PICKLE TOW

There was an auld wife had a wee pickle tow,
And she would gae try the spinning o't,
But louten her down, her rock took a low,
And that was an ill beginning o't!
She lap and she grat, she slet and she slang,
She trow and she drew, she ringled, she rang,
She choaked she bocked and cried, Let me hang,
That ever I try'd the spinning o't.

I hae been a wife these threescore of years,
And never did try the spinning o't;
But how I was sarked foul fa' them that spears,
For it minds me o' the beginnin o't;
The women now a-days are turned fae bra',
That ilk ane maun hae a sark, some maun hae twa,
But the warld was better whan seint ane ava,
But a wee rag at the beginning o't.

Foul fa' them that e'er advis'd me to spin,
For it minds me o' the beginning o't;
I might well have ended as I had begun,
And never had try'd the beginning o't;
But they say she's a wise wife wha kens her ain weird;

I thought ance a day it wad never be speir'd,
How loot you the low tak the rock by the beard,
Whan you gaed to try the spinning o't?

The spinning, the spinning, it gars my heart fab,
Whan I think on the beginning o't;
I thought ance in a day to 'ave made a wab,
And this was to 'ave been the beginning o't;
But had I nine daughters, as I hae but three,
The safest and soundest advice I wad gie,
That they frae spinning wad keep their hands free,
For fear o' an ill beginning o't.

But in spit of my counsel it they wad needs run
The dreary sad task o' the spinning o't,
Let them seekout a loun place at the heat o' the fun,
Syne venture on the beginning o':
For, O do as I've done, alake and vow,
To busk up a rock at the cheek of a low,
They'd say, that I had little wit in my pow,
And as little I've done wi' the spinning o't.

Turning to the dance associated with 'The Roke and the Wee Pickle Tow', it does not seem possible to trace any information as to its origins. In *Book 3* of the Royal Scottish Country Dance Society it is listed in the company of the 'Foursome Reel' and the 'Reel of Tulloch', which might suggest a measure of antiquity.

DANCE – THE ROKE AND THE WEE PICKLE TOW – 32 BAR JIG

Bars

1 – 4	First couple cross over giving right hands and cast off one place.
5 – 6	First couple turn to own sides with left hands.
7 – 8	Give right hand and lead up to top and finish facing down the dance.
9 – 12	First and second couples, four hands round,
13 – 16	and back again.
17 – 20	First couple lead down the middle,
21 – 24	and up again.
25 – 32	First and second couples *poussette*. Repeat having passed a couple.

Tune: 'The Roke and the Wee Pickle Tow'.

Linlithgow Reed Band

Linlithgow Reed Band are very much part of the town and the town in return is affectionate towards them. Their red tunics, military bearing and positive music, not to mention the kentspeckle figure of conductor Jo Lavery at their head, seem to be part of every special occasion in Linlithgow, be it in church, marquee or the High Street. They have a style of their own.

To seek the roots of the Reed Band we must go back to 1954 when for some reason or other the Kinneil Reed Band, which had been founded in 1858, decided to drop their reed section and become the Kinneil Silver Band. Understandably this decision was not well received by the unwanted reed section who, with spirit, decided to form a new band, the Linlithgow Reed Band. Then came a stroke of luck for Linlithgow, if not for a little place on the road to Edinburgh. The Winchburgh Silver Band fell upon difficult times, their solo cornet player agreed to join the new Linlithgow Band, and he was followed by a dozen others, most possessing their own instruments. A band committee came into being, including such major figures of the town as Arthur (Pop) Brown of the *Gazette* as secretary and Willie Oliphant the baker as treasurer. The band's first concert was held on 6 May 1956. The MC was David Morrison, namesake father of a much respected figure in the town today. The cornet solo that day was 'Bless This House' played by Eric Cook, and that tune was appropriately played at his funeral in St Ninian's Church.

The initial priority for the band was finding somewhere to practise. The Coleman brothers had bought the old co-operative hall and allowed the band its use for storage and practice on condition the place was tidied up after each rehearsal. But the hall was earmarked for demolition and the search for new premises had to be begun. Fund raising got under way, mainly with whist drives and bingo. The band's next home was to be in the former, and by then unused, Kelly's Model Lodging House. This involved a cleaning-up job before rehearsals could commence. Worse still, the wood burning fires that were lit to warm the area on practice nights belched an indecent amount of smoke into both the practice area and an adjoining shop. The old Craigmailen Church Hall provided a temporary home until a private developer appeared and forced the band to move to Laetare Hostel, where they stayed until 1980. Then, with the help of then-councillor Jimmy McGinley, property was obtained on council ground, to be shared with the town's Pipe Band. One can imagine the sense of relief that the band must have felt.

With a shortage of funds the obtaining of uniforms was also a problem. Initially a deal seems to have been done with a statutory transport body keen to get rid of some surplus-to-requirement jackets. Unfortunately the dye from the red band affixed to the sleeves had a habit of running onto shirts when conditions were wet. Maroon blazers were adopted and continued in use until 1993, when the very recognisable red jackets and black trousers with red band and gold braid were purchased. A year or two later, hats made their appearance, endorsing the military look of the band.

The Reed Band's first appearance at the Marches was in 1956. It was perhaps not as auspicious an introduction as it might have been. The Kinneil Band had led the Marches prior to the War and then up to 1955, and were a much respected band. As the Linlithgow Reed Band approached the Provost's House that 1956 Marches morning, some local diehards were in position wielding a petition saying the band was not fit for the job. There had been an unfortunate Deacons Night that May when, as some of the members had never played while marching before, it was decided the band would stand and play for the first two turns round the well, before circling for the third turn. This action did not receive understanding from the natives of the town and a critical poem about it was printed in the *Gazette*. Who would, or could, pass such a comment today? The Band, incidentally, traditionally starts Marches Day with the playing of the hymn tune 'Crimmond', in memory of former members.

There are few Marches that do not produce a story or two. There is the tale of one new band member who attended his first Marches morning breakfast, which at the time was held in Longcroft Hall. It was the custom for the Ladies Committee to serve bacon rolls and one lady distributed a large box of biscuits round the younger members of the band. However, unknown to the new member, some of the young people had been trying out his trombone and the band had reached the 'Brig' before it was discovered the instrument was choked with crunched biscuit.

The Reed Band is seen regularly in Linlithgow. One thinks of it particularly in connection with the Marches, and its Christmas and spring concerts in St Michael's Church. In the area it is a regular at a host of gala days, the Queensferry Raft Race and the Free Colliers' celebration in August. One should also mention its presence in the Edinburgh Cavalcade, which marks the beginning of the Edinburgh Festival. And the world outwith the local area must not be forgotten: the band has performed from Moffat to Inverness.

The Reed Band has a special association with the Hochsauerland in Germany, with which West Lothian is twinned, and has travelled there to perform on three occasions. In 1999, the Band returned to Germany to perform in and around Koblenz and the Rhine area, before moving on to Luxembourg.

After many years devoted to military service and music, Jo Lavery accepted the

Jo Lavery, prior to his retirement as conductor of the Reed Band

post of conductor of the Band in 1985. But Jo decided that with the band getting ready to celebrate the ripe age of fifty years in 2006 it was time for him to put down the baton and he made his final appearance on the podium at the Spring concert that year. The band's Golden Jubilee has been and is being celebrated in many ways. Martine Stead of the Folk Festival Association designed a new logo for the band which may be seen not only on the band's new casual wear T and sweat shirts but on the new drum presented by the Fraternity of Dyers and the music stand banners donated by the Deacon's Court. A ceilidh ball is to be held in September with invitations going to founder members and representatives of bands with which the Reed Band has had a connection.

Six weeks is not a long time for a band to practice a completely new programme but that was the time given to Marco Marzella, the band's new conductor, to prepare for his first concert. And it was a special concert as it was a joint one with the distinguished Kinneil Silver Band. The two bands complemented each other perfectly on stage and the pleasure of playing together extended into the social held after the concert.

The range of instruments in the Reed Band is wide, it is in effect an orchestra without strings. Long may we in the town enjoy its company.

Quern

Linlithgow-based Quern is probably Scotland's most widely travelled traditionally inclined amateur music group. In Scotland, the group has performed from Ullapool in the north to Eyemouth in the south. Abroad, they have taken the stage from Vancouver Island in the west to Moscow in the east and Sydney in the south. Such travels were never envisaged when the group first struggled to find its niche in the market.

Quern

Quern's story starts in the autumn of 1984 when, during the interval of a country dance club evening in Chalmers Hall, five members pondered over how they might find more live music for dancing to, rather than having to rely on their records, which were showing signs of age. To the question, 'Could we do it ourselves?', which came from the one dancer recognised as a musician, were a variety of responses: 'I have a fiddle under the bed but haven't touched it for 25 years.' 'I can play hymn tunes on the piano.' 'I might manage a few chords.' 'I have a drum in the attic.' Amidst giggles, a practice was arranged. It took the optimistic five nearly six weeks to play four tunes at the right tempo for dancing. Such was the pride, not to say amazement, at the achievement, the group gave itself a name. One of the two pianists jettisoned his keyboard (legless, it had sat on a tartan blanket which concealed an ironing board) and started to learn bass guitar. Music making was now to be taken seriously.

There was a local decision taken that Linlithgow would have a festival in 1985. Quern was enthusiastic about taking part but wished to present something distinctive. The writer had at that time prepared a number of talks on Scottish literary figures which he was giving as an entertainment to a range of organisations. It was decided to take the prepared talk on 'Hogg – the Ettrick Shepherd' and integrate into its script a range of Hogg's songs. This prompted two splendid singers to join the group, with a flautist arriving shortly afterwards. The Hogg presentation was extremely well received, the late Tom McGovern referring to it in the *Gazette* as 'a pearl at the centre of the festival'. This success encouraged other talks to be adapted into musical presentations and these, along with concerts, allowed Quern to develop a distinct personality. The success also prompted the group's objectives, which had now been clearly set, and these were, and still are:

> to promote the music and culture of Scotland in a lively and imaginative way, and operating on an expenses only basis, to act as a vehicle for non-commercial organisations in their fund raising activities.

The descriptive term used in the group's publicity of 'music – mainly in the Scottish Idiom' permits musical forays into fields other than Scottish for about 20 per cent of the programme, something which allows the group to play to its strengths and which is welcomed by audiences. The demand for the group grew and a regular round of visits to homes, hospitals, churches and halls made for a busy life in and around Linlithgow and Edinburgh. One concert in Livingston still draws smiles when recalled. As the singer was giving his all to Burns' 'A Red, Red Rose' a dog meandered down the centre aisle and started sniffing his trouser legs. The atmosphere was electric, but it decided just to sit across his feet and enjoy the vocal.

Quern took part in a *Festival d'Histoire* in Guyancourt in 1987 and returned to play in the twin town two years later. This time though the journey was extended, first with an attendance at the St Malo Festival, then by several minor Brittany festivals.

The writer had scripted and produced a musical presentation on the life of Robert Service, the poet and chronicler of the Klondike gold rush. Service had lived for many years in Lancieaux in Brittany where he had been a considerable benefactor to the town, and the town decided to present a *Hommage à Robert Service* in his honour. It was to be quite a day, with wreath laying and Ambassadorial and academic speeches, culminating in Quern's show *Life of Service* – in French, be it noted, for which a team of nine translators had been gathered together. Much sweat was in evidence as scripts and verses and songs were practised and presented in French.

The following year saw Quern based in Germany performing in West Lothian's twin province of Hochsauerlandkreis. 1992 was an eventful year as Quern joined the Dunedin Dancers from Edinburgh to take part in an International Dance Festival in Ruurlo in Holland; the ferry caught fire and members sat up all night in the ship's lounge wearing lifejackets. For the first time on stage the group faced a four figure audience.

Quern was now helping charities in their fund raising efforts across a wide swathe of Central Scotland. But 1994, the 10th anniversary year, was to be special.

Over a six week period every year the Orangerie in Strasbourg presents, as a tourist attraction, a different international music group every night to a non-paying audience. Quern accepted an invitation to attend. It was one of those special nights when the group could do no wrong, receiving a tremendous reception from an audience accustomed to seeing some of the best amateur talent in the world. The next day's performance in the Strasbourg Parliament was the icing on the cake.

Return visits would now be paid to Guyancourt and Lancieux but it was the invitations coming from various Scots and Burns Societies in Australia that were causing the excitement. A tour was agreed for 1999 and the highlights were many. A Burns performance on Bondi Beach Pavilion, the group's *Linlithgow Story* in the town of Lithgow, attendance at a Naturalisation ceremony and the joy of giving expats a link with home. And the coach that arrived to pick up the group with the appropriate number of seats but no space for instruments and luggage will not soon be forgotten.

Mention should be made here of Quern's attendance at the Edinburgh Festival Fringe. There is no doubt the Fringe was good to, and for, Quern. While the average audience size for Fringe shows is around twenty, Quern was averaging some years around the two hundred mark. The main venue used was St Mark's Unitarian Church. One night when the hall was almost full an agitated lady was seen running around. When asked if anything was wrong she explained, 'My two coaches haven't arrived yet.' They did arrive, although how their occupants were crammed in is a mystery.

One particular show warrants a mention. Specially written for the occasion, *The Story of Country Dancing* was supported by dancers from all over Central Scotland. The Dunedin Dancers in their special regalia were the perfect partners to Quern.

The group's attendance at the Fringe brought Quern to the attention of a wide audience and resulted in many invitations to perform forth of their home ground. Spain, in 2000, was added to the overseas travel list, with a series of concerts in and around Gerona.

Quern had been aware for some time of the dearth of Scottish country dance bands in Western Canada and it was no surprise when a friend-of-a-friend type of invitation reached the group. Allied to this was interest shown in the group's musical presentations by the Scottish Cultural Centre in Vancouver. Quern's first Canadian tour was a marvellous experience with incredible receptions. To see on arriving at a hall a sign declaring 'Sorry – Sold Out' is a tremendous morale booster. As was the number of return invitations received before leaving the country.

While maintaining their round of concerts at home on behalf of charities, churches and non-commercial organisations, Quern had been adjusting their musical arrangements. Group singing became more prominent and dancing was introduced, some of the dances being devised for specific occasions by a group member. These refinements paid off handsomely on 2002's Highland and Bavarian tours. And they went down well in Russia.

In 2003, West Lothian council received an invitation to send traditional musicians to a Scottish Festival held on a regular basis in Moscow. Quern and Linlithgow Folk Festival Association accepted the council's nomination to attend. Although frequently in contact, the two groups appeared mainly at different venues. Regarded by many in the group as their greatest experience with Quern, they travelled the 500 kilometres to Lipetsk, with a police escort much of the way, to share the stage with the Cossack State Dance Company before an audience of almost 5,000. The ovations, the bouquets, being the guests of honour at banquets, the enthusiasm of the Russian people for Scottish music, have all left an indelible memory with the group. Being described by the organiser as 'the best ambassadors from Scotland in the seven years of the festival' made what was undoubtedly a gruelling tour well worth while. The following year, 2004, saw Quern return, first to Guyancourt to take part in a Burns Supper, and then to Vancouver and Vancouver Island. Again it was a series of sell out concerts.

The big event of 2005 was the group's tour in Kenya. The origins of that tour, which can only be described as exciting from start to finish, lay in a performance given by Quern in Linlithgow the previous year. This was attended by two Kenyans on holiday who, impressed by the entertainment given thought the group might be a useful vehicle in helping them raise funds for Nanyuki Cottage Hospital in Kenya with which they were associated. The Kenyans applied themselves with tremendous vigour to make the necessary arrangements on their return, pursuing support from all quarters. The tour was a tremendous success, both in financial terms – as a consequence a new laboratory for the hospital has now been built – and for the enjoyment of those in Kenya who have little opportunity to enjoy live Scottish music. The venues ranged from places with international reputations to a marquee erected in the bush in an area largely lit by flares. Special mention must be made of the night time concert given in the 15th century Fort Jesus in Mombassa and the concert given in the Muthaiga Club so authentically associated with Karen Blixen, the author of the book *Out of Africa*.

January 2006 saw Quern take part in the twinning associations' Burns Supper in Pignitz, Bavaria, before they continued on to give a concert in the Czech Republic. Their new musical presentation 'The Auld Alliance' was launched in May and was performed in French at six different locations in France in October of this year. Particularly interesting was their appearance at the Scots Kirk in Paris, where the minister, the Rev. Alan Millar, served at one time as the assistant minister in St Michaels.

A major event in the town every year is the Quern Fiddlers' Rally, in conjunction with Linlithgow Grange Rotary, when around seventy musicians from the Dunkeld and Angus Strathspey and Reel Societies in the north, to The Borders Society in the south, take the stage to raise funds for local charities. The rally, part of the town's lead up to the Riding of the Marches, has been a tremendous success since its inception ten years ago, commanding large audiences and raising substantial funds for local charities.

Linlithgow Arts Guild

The contribution the Arts Guild makes to the cultural life of the town is quite tremendous, and it operates in no narrow field, as a perusal of its programmes will show. Opera companies and ensembles, guitar players and pianists, choirs and brass bands, duos, trios and quartets all seek to satisfy the demand for such entertainment as exists in the town. From the end of September to April the Arts Guild makes its presence felt. It is one of those organisations which came to life almost by accident.

In 1968, the Linlithgow town council decided that two weeks should be set aside for culture in the town, focusing on music, drama and visual art. It was intended it should be an event of some standing and it was fortunate that significant people in their fields agreed to become involved. Robert Ponsonby (later Sir Robert), the then Director of the Edinburgh International Festival, offered his services; Allen Wright and Conrad Wilson, the drama and music critics of the *Scotsman*, also became involved. And fortunate indeed was the willingness of Richard Demarco to arrange an art exhibition in the Burgh Halls which included two of his own paintings, one of which found a permanent home in the town. Lectures, seminars and workshops were all fitted in and the event was an outstanding success.

Julia Wade, the Honorary President of the Arts Guild, tells of the next step which led to its formation. In conversation with Robert Ponsonby she was asked why she didn't start an Arts Guild in the town. In response to her claim she wouldn't know where to begin, Ponsonby, a man who obviously believed in starting at the top, suggested inviting the Scottish National Orchestra, or at least half of it – the other half, he said, could go somewhere else. Jest or not, that was what happened six months later, when an audience of five hundred filled the Academy Hall to hear a popular orchestral programme. Fired with enthusiasm, a public meeting was called and the decision was taken to form an Arts Guild. The programme for that first 1969–70 season indicates the amount of work that had been done behind the scenes. It included theatre, opera, two recitals, a talk and a return visit by half of the Scottish National Orchestra. One is inclined to say, 'the rest is history'.

Catastrophes large and small abound in any organisation; hopefully most of them finish up as amusing anecdotes. One, which has come the writer's way, concerns an orchestra that appeared some years ago under a German conductor. The concert was being held in the Academy and in the middle of some serious music, to the consternation of the office-bearers at least, the bell indicating the end of a school period broke into its penetrating ring. Bravely the conductor battled on. Later attempts to express apologies were rejected by the conductor, who accused the organisers of being barbarians. At the next concert, the organiser sought out the janitor to ensure all the arrangements were in order. 'Aye they are,' he nodded, and turning to his side kick continued, 'it's the Arts Guild the nicht, remember, nae bells.' Such is life.

The Arts Guild was now well under way. It has always been policy that only professional musicians and artistes should be engaged, in an attempt to combine quality with box office appeal. From the very beginning the Guild received financial support from the Scottish Arts Council and for this to continue it had to be shown that proper concert promotion was being undertaken. It has been possible to maintain the very high standards set, initially by getting sponsorship from the local council and generous local firms, and through continued support from Music Enterprise Scotland.

There not being a proper concert hall in Linlithgow, the Arts Guild tries to match venues, artistes and potential audience numbers. St Michael's Church, with its superb acoustics and capacious if rather uncomfortable seating, is used for choral visits, orchestral concerts and popular events. Some concerts are held in the Academy, which has banked seating, while quartets and the like are placed in the primary school now that audiences have outgrown the Kirk Hall. There is a continuing hope that some day a benefactor will appear with lottery money to build a concert hall – something the town needs rather badly.

The Arts Guild programme has become more focussed on concerts as other organisations in the town have developed to meet the demand for different art forms. There are normally seven or eight concerts during the winter season, plus a film evening jointly promoted with the Film Society, a musical coffee morning, and a further concert or entertainment after the AGM. Membership varies year by year according to the popularity of the programme, and may reach the 150 mark. Visitors usually swell the audience numbers by a further 50 to a 100, drawn from all over the Central Belt. The Arts Guild continues to hold its own against competition from the bright lights of Edinburgh and Glasgow.

Top class artistes from all over the world have appeared at the Arts Guild, frequently as part of wider tours of Scotland. Recent performers include groups from Moscow, Prague, Berlin and Japan. The policy is simply to secure the best affordable professionals to perform in the town. Efforts are made to book young performers who might go on to become household names. Winners of the Scottish 'Tunnell Trust' prize have been very impressive, and previous 'young' performers have included Hinge and Bracket, James Galway and Evelyn Glennie, all at early stages in their careers. Many will remember the Guild's 25th anniversary in October 1994, when St Michael's Church was the venue for Elgar's 'Kingdom', performed by the Scottish Sinfonia and Choir and conducted by Neil Mantle, later to be associated with the BBC Scottish Symphony Orchestra and the Scottish National Orchestra. The Guild's 35th anniversary was marked with a piano recital by Linlithgow's own international star, Steven Osborne.

The Chairman's report presented in April again confirmed the leading position of the Linlithgow Arts Guild in terms of membership numbers and audience support. Much of this must be due to the quality and diversity of the programmes offered. Looking ahead one senses anticipation in particular for the Scottish Opera's fully staged performance of Strauss's 'Die Fledermaus' and mention must be made of the interest engendered by Linlithgow film-maker Iain Walker's new award-winning film on the Scottish connections of Edvard Grieg whose forebears made the leap from Aberdeenshire to Norway.

From his home in Linlithgow, Steven Osborne flies to concert venues all over the world. Recognised as one of the United Kingdom's most talented, individualistic and sought after pianists, his allegiance to his home town has never faltered. The piano being a favourite toy from earliest days, Osborne commenced lessons at the age of five. At Linlithgow Primary School his talent was recognised by headmaster William Henry, who had the young pupil play at morning assembly. By the age of ten he had appeared on Glen Michael's *Cavalcade*, a Sunday afternoon STV programme some mature readers may remember. Around this time he took part in a competition and the judicator commented he should apply for admission to a specialist music school. Success came his way and his time at St Mary's Music School in Edinburgh was followed by graduation with first class honours in the joint degree course from Manchester University and the Royal Northern College of Music in Manchester. He later took a Master's degree from the Royal Northern College.

Nationally, Osborne came to prominence when, in 1998, he came second in the piano section of the BBC Young Musician of the Year competition. Then, in 1991, he won first prize in the Clara Haskill competition. He took part in many festivals, made a highly acclaimed debut in the Wigmore Hall in 1994, and the same week won the Edward Boyle Award. His serious travels were now to begin as he made appearances in Japan and in the United States after winning the Naumburg International Piano competition in New York. Press reports on his concerts acknowledged his brilliance. At home he appeared as soloist with such major orchestras as the BBC Symphony Orchestra and the Hallé. His regular perform-ances at the Edinburgh Festival have given local audiences an opportunity to appreciate his worth, and he has now played five times at 'the Proms'. Here one would mention his televised rendering of Gershwin's 'Rhapsody in Blue' with the BBC Symphony Orchestra, which was given the highest praise by critics. On the international circuit, he has performed with orchestras ranging from the Bergen and Munich Philharmonics to the Finnish Radio and Lahti Symphony Orchestras and various American orchestras. Concert appearances include such venues as the Kennedy Centre in Washington, Suntory Hall in Tokyo, the Konzerthaus in Vienna and the Philharmonie in Berlin. The list of prestigious venues seems endless. His diary includes future performances at Carnegie Hall in New York and the Palais des Beaux Arts in Brussels. Yet, busy as his schedule is, Osborne has always found time to perform in his home town and has delighted members of the Arts Guild on many occasions. On stage he likes to make contact with his audience and is not afraid to speak to them directly, commenting on the various pieces in his programme. He believes strongly in the art of improvisation and this may explain his great love for jazz. Indeed he has been known to give a classical concert and a jazz concert on the same night. That says much for his stamina, which some may put down to his love of hill-walking.

Linlithgow Amateur Musical Productions

There are many clubs and associations in Linlithgow. One wonders if any town in Scotland can match it for such intensity. Where a demand for an activity is identified, it always seems that some individual or group will seek to satisfy it. In 1985 a feeling arose that the town should have a society to offer its worthy citizens musical shows. The inevitable advertisement was placed in the *Gazette*, a meeting room was booked in the Academy, some forty people turned up, and the decision was taken. No longer would enthusiasts have to make for the theatres of Edinburgh, Glasgow and London. Linlithgow would host the best of musical shows.

Before rushing into its first musical comedy, the newly formed Linlithgow Amateur Musical Productions (LAMP) organised a modest concert in Queen Margaret's Hall. This would allow them to raise money for the first musical, make the public aware of what they intended doing, and 'blood' those with no experience in 'treading the boards'. The night provided an encouraging start. The first song performed was 'The Night They Invented Champagne'. A few bottles were popped at the end of the evening.

The society's first full show was *Oklahoma*, which was received with wide acclaim. But it brought home to new members the extent of the work involved. Everyone knew a musical requires a cast. What had not been so widely anticipated was the number of other bodies required – people were needed to design and prepare costumes and backdrops, sell tickets, obtain musicians, order scores, and perform all the other important roles involved in staging a full musical production. Learning about all these things was at times a little painful. But the proof of the pudding is in the eating, and LAMP has built up an enviable reputation over the past 25 years. It is worthwhile reminding ourselves of the shows that have been performed:

Oklahoma	My Fair Lady
The Merry Widow	The King and I
Hello Dolly	Pirates of Penzance
South Pacific	Carousel
Brigadoon	Oliver
Anything Goes	The Pyjama Game
The Sound of Music	Annie
Guys and Dolls	Calamity Jane
Mame	Kiss Me Kate
Fiddler on the Roof	

The introduction of children into theatre life has been taken very seriously. The Children's Theatre was founded in 1995. Rehearsals begin in November, with shows scheduled for the school's Easter holiday. Around 50 young people between the ages of nine and fifteen are likely to perform. With enthusiasm high, there can be much competition for a place. Sadly the Academy theatre's stage is not infinite in size. Again, the Children's Theatre has achieved much success, and perhaps more importantly, it has introduced many youngsters to the pleasures of music and song and widened their knowledge of the genre, the benefits of which will stay with them over the years. Children's Theatre productions include:

The Wizard of Oz	The Boyfriend
Oklahoma	Bugsy Malone
Anything Goes	The King and I
Oliver	Brigadoon
Smike	

Linlithgow Folk Festival Association

Folk Festival Folk

The aims of the Linlithgow Folk Festival Association as set out in its constitution are clear and to the point. They are:

> To plan and implement an annual folk festival.
> To organise and promote an annual programme of events and activities.
> To provide an opportunity for local musicians to participate and develop their skills within the folk medium through sessions and workshops.

While these aims indicate the professionalism that has come to be associated with the Association, it cannot be said that its origins were quite so tidy. Grace McClure, who has led the way from her position of chairperson for the first six years, tells how she had conversations with friends in 1998 about staging a folk festival. Opening a local paper one day, she read a positive but unexpected head-line: the town was going to have such an event. More than that, West Lothian council was making encouraging noises. With her name to the fore, Grace decided on action. A meeting was called in the early part of 1999, a committee was formed, a constitution agreed, and the decision taken to hold a festival that year. Little grass was being allowed to grow. Along with some money from the council, very considerable professional support was given during the first year and this eased the load considerably for the volunteers.

For many years, Nora Devine was the focus of the folk scene in Linlithgow, and she was able to point the committee in the direction of artistes likely to support the new festival. Sadly she died just a week before the first festival was held. A few months later, a special concert in her memory was held. It featured the McCalmans, who were the first group to appear in the folk club she formed. She has been well remembered in folk circles over the years.

The first festival made tremendous impact in the town. Around 150 attended the concert, which featured Eddie Walker and Itchy Fingers. A similar number of people participated in various hostelries. Fiddle, guitar, step dance and song harmony workshops were held and the Reel Ale Céilidh Band led the Friday night céilidh. The first AGM report from the chair bubbled with enthusiasm.

We can discern at this time the committee's strong desire to involve and encourage musicians – especially local musicians – irrespective of their ability level, and to this end monthly sessions were started. Putting on entertainment for the general public has never been seen as the be-all and end-all of the Association's work. The Association is committed to taking music to people who cannot attend concerts, for example residents in old folk's homes. The Association is also active in the community, providing music for Burns Suppers and local events.

Such was the impact of the first festival in traditional music circles, the issued programme for the second featured artistes of national standing such as Gordeanna McCulloch and Ceolbeg. Local involvement in the shape of Sangschule and the Reed and Pipe Bands was strong, and this has continued over the years. Receipt of a lottery grant allowed the Association to expand their work by holding a series of winter workshops relating to the traditional music field, classes being held in whistle, bodhran and mixed instruments.

The year 2001 proved beyond doubt that the Association's festival was now a major event, as Brian McNeill and Stravaig provided the top of the bill. Brian McNeill's standing has since been recognised by his appointment to head of traditional music at the Royal Scottish Academy of Music and Drama. Also appearing that year was Mairi Campbell, surely one of the most talented individuals in the music field in Scotland. A brilliant fiddler, viola player and singer, Mairi confined herself to promoting the resurgent step dance on this occasion.

It was about this time that Grace McClure paid a visit to Stirling folk club, where the great Tom Paxton was appearing. Approaching him after the concert, using her considerable charm Grace bravely invited him to perform in Linlithgow. It was not easily arranged but success eventually came. A 2002 poster promoting a Tom Paxton tour, shows – beneath venues in Cardiff, London, Manchester and Glasgow – the perhaps not so well known venue of Linlithgow Academy.

The year leading up to the fourth festival saw increasing contacts being made with folk clubs across Scotland. It was a two way gain. It kept the Association outward-looking and it encouraged musicians from elsewhere to attend and perhaps host sessions in the town. The brainchild of Association stalwart Murdoch Kennedy, a big and popular step forward around this time was the inception of special Matt McGinn nights, when up to thirty performers took the stage to honour the memory of one of Scotland's greatest musical sons. And the Association made its first overseas journey to Linlithgow's twin town of Guyancourt – a connection that would become ever more expansive and entertaining over the years. Along with the all-ladies group, the Poozies, the 2002 festival saw an increasing number of workshops, the introduction of country dancing, and a songwriters' concert taking place in Blackness, the old port of Linlithgow.

Innovation came to the fore the following year as the Association took to the Union Canal on musical cruises. The festival céilidh was a packed out event, Gordeanna McCulloch and Mairi Campbell paid return visits, while bluegrass

A Session in Progress at the Black Bitch

enthusiasts had a field day. But the man they all came to see was Eric Bogle, the Australian Scot from the Borders whose anti-war songs such as 'The Green Fields of France' and 'The Band Played Waltzing Matilda' can be heard in all the English speaking countries of the world. For some members of the Association the main memory of the year will be their visit to the Scottish Festival in Moscow with Quern. Gathering some local musicians together for the event under the highly entertaining Neil Macdonald, the Black Bitch Band came into being. This band has now become firmly entrenched in the local scene, and has made a CD, which includes a wonderfully provocative song called 'Cockleroi'. Glenn Muir provided the lyrics, with Neil Macdonald composing the music.

The Association again showed its willingness to break new ground in 2004, when the first item on the programme was an illustrated talk by the eminent literary figure Dr Fred Freeman on 'Burns as a Songwriter'. The Scottish Bluegrass Association had a field day in Laetare, their workshops being followed by the appearance of the United States Guitar Champion Steve Kaufman (instrumental competitions are standard practice in North America). Sunday saw a Gospel session, and the main Saturday concert focused on the Sangsters and the very up-and-coming Back of the Moon.

September 2005 saw the charismatic Ralph McTell head the bill at the Folk Festival and enjoy the company of local musicians in the Black Bitch Tavern afterwards. Members of the family of Matt McGinn turned up at the Burgh Halls in March to see the effort being made in Linlithgow to keep the memory of the songwriter alive while Eric Bogle paid his second visit to Linlithgow. This time though his concert was linked to entertainment leading to the Marches, something we can expect to see extended in the future.

The organisers of the Linlithgow Folk Festival have a certain eye for an opening and the 480th anniversary of the Battle of Linlithgow Bridge seemed to them to be an opportunity for songwriters to display their talents. So, not only did the 2006 Folk Festival include a lecture on the intrigues and warfare of the Clans and Families that sought to dominate the young King James v, but West Lothian Songwriters group and others commemorated the battle with original material.

On two occasions in particular the Association has pulled out all the stops to create an entertainment that was special. In 2003, when the Guyancourt contingent arrived for their visit, the Association provided a highly entertaining musical presentation on all the events to be found in Linlithgow in the course of a year. Inevitably, there was a request for more of the same. Two years later, with 'Folk – Folk From Other Airts', they embarked on a musical tour around Scotland illustrating our cultural differences. It was another success story.

Linlithgow Scottish Country Dance Club

In August of 1980, in response to an advertisement in the *Gazette*, over 20 enthusiasts attended a meeting in the Burgh Halls to make the decision that the town should have its own Country Dance Club. The next month saw dancing start in Chalmers Hall. In November, well over a hundred dancers made for the Academy for the new club's first formal dance, the music being supplied by Jack Stalker's Band. Justifiably, there was a feeling of pride in the club.

Organisations develop their own personality and the fledging club was no exception. The committee knew what it wanted. It was to be a social club with emphasis on dancing, rather than a class where dances were taught. This friendly approach (not to mention the club's splendid suppers) paid dividends, and before long a core of dancers from all over Central Scotland were making for Chalmers Hall on Friday nights, and bringing their friends to the more formal dances in other venues in the town. There was live music provided by country dance bands roughly once a month, with records filling in the rest of the time.

In those early years, new or less well known dances were walked through in the first half of the Friday evening session, then – after the inevitable cup of tea and a biscuit – those that people were expected to know already were danced with very little instruction. It could be awkward when newcomers with no dancing experience turned up, but the club's reputation in the town for friendliness was well deserved and before long the novices' toes were twinkling with the rest. It was club practice to allow visitors three Friday night visits before suggesting they take out membership. In fact, most joined on their first visit to Chalmers Hall.

Most country dance clubs like to have a few dances in the year that are regarded as special. The Hogmany Jig was an early introduction that has stood the test of time. What better way is there to bid the Old Year *adieu* than to dance it out? In 1984 came the End-of-Season Dance, and a Marches Dance with the Provost in attendance also springs to mind. An Annual Ball gave the ladies the opportunity to show off their finery, and the ballroom of Hopetoun House provided a special, if expensive, ambience for the club on a few occasions. The Burgh Halls were often used, the floor there being considered kinder to dancers' feet than that at the Academy. People like to dance in places with character, and for a few years eyes had been focused on the palace. To get permission to dance there was not easy but it was ultimately forthcoming, and in the 1980s the ambition was satisfied. John Carsewell's Scotch Hop is now a regular event there, and is referred to elsewhere in the book.

For many years the club, in company with the West Lothian Branch of the

Royal Scottish Country Dance Society and the Kirkliston and South Queensferry Clubs, has raised substantial funds for charity at a special dance. Club nights at Christmas often involve members showing off their talents, and one remembers with a laugh the four Morris dancers who appeared with jingling bells one year to have the place in hysterics.

Today the club has a core of very good dancers who are more than capable of improving the general quality of the dancing, but in earlier years there was frequently the suggestion that the attendance of a qualified teacher might be beneficial. This was not always a happy introduction. One remembers the arrival of a most charming lady from Edinburgh who – it must have been through strength of character – forced the mature ladies of the club into a series of leg exercises. These included ballet *pliés*, bending the legs while keeping the back erect. The groans were frightening; the inelegance made many a gentleman look away.

As a club, there has always been a desire to be involved in town and indeed West Lothian happenings. It is good citizenship and it is good for the promotion of our native culture. This generally means demonstrating some of our country dances.

An early recollection is of a demonstration that did not follow the normal elegant pattern. It took place in the Academy when the club accepted an invitation to dance at a concert. Dressed in a motley collection of what might be termed holiday clothes, with the odd beer bottle protruding from a pocket, a rowdy bevy of dancers took the floor to dance, much to the delight of the audience, 'Rothesay at the Fair'. But appropriate costumes have been put on for many special occasions; the Advent Fair and enactments in the palace are good examples. The regular bread and butter demonstrations centre on homes and hospitals, fêtes and charity occasions, town events and Burns Suppers. One could go on and on. Such attendances can have their moments, and a favourite anecdote is about the team that went to dance at a charity fund-raising event. Attention had concentrated on making sure all the audience would see the dancing. Attention had not been paid to the surroundings. The first dance involved a 'down the middle and up' movement followed by a *poussette*. Only when the music and dancing started was it realised that the dancers were directly in line with a set of automatic doors which, with a noise of their own, kept opening and closing – but not in time to the music.

Pride of place as a deviser of dances in the club must go to Heather Knox who, many claim, never forgets a dance. Her 'Double H' collection makes her talents clear.

Turning to bands, for many years Jack Stalker was the automatic choice. A splendid fiddler, Jack and his most likeable crew were firm friends of the club and could always be relied on to get the right fit of tunes and dances. But as members took to visiting other clubs there inevitably came an urge to dance to other bands, and with the club's substantial reputation for good dancing and happy evenings, top bands were more than happy to oblige. Bobby Crowe – who was recording substantially for the Royal Scottish Country Dance Society at the time – gave an immaculate performance, Jack Delaney was high in the popularity stakes, while Gordon Shand was and is always sure of a warm welcome. From the locality, Fidra Céilidh Band and Quern have contributed to the club scene.

Country dancing in Princes Street Gardens is always a sure way to attract and entertain visitors to the capital city. For the first time in the summer of 2005 dancers from the club took part along with dancers from other dance clubs in the Edinburgh area. As ever the Hogmany Jig in Linlithgow was popular and well attended but the most important social occasion of the year was undoubtedly the 25th anniversary ball held in the Academy. Attended by the President of the Royal Scottish Country Dance Society and representatives of a large number of clubs it was, as they say, a glittering affair and worthy of the occasion.

CHAPTER 5

A Walk around St Michael's Parish Church

St Michael's Parish Church, with its Crown of Thorns

ST MICHAEL'S CHURCH, one of the most historic and beautiful churches in Scotland, is a focal point in Linlithgow life. Like its namesakes, the Church of St Michael's Mount in Cornwall and the sky-reaching tower of Mont St Michel in France, it exerts a magnetic pull on camera-wielding visitors. The name 'Michael' does not sound particularly Biblical, and indeed there is scant reference to a St Michael in the Bible until we come to Daniel and Revelation Chapter 12, where we read:

> Then there was war in heaven; Michael and the angels under his command fought the dragon and his hosts of fallen angels. And the dragon lost the battle and was

forced from heaven. This great dragon, the ancient serpent called the devil, or Satan, the one deceiving the whole world – was thrown down on to the earth with all his army.

Michaelmas, a September date that was much used at one time in Scotland in farm tenancy agreements, is said to be the anniversary of the dedication of a Church of St Michael on the Salarian Way from Rome to Ancona in the sixth century. Coming nearer to home we remember that St Michael has been adopted as the patron saint of our Ancient and Royal Burgh, and he figures in the town's motto: 'St Michael is kind to strangers.'

Like all churches dedicated to St Michael, the one in Linlithgow is built on raised ground. It is one of the finest examples of a medieval church in Scotland. When the site was first used for religious purposes we do not know. It has been suggested its origins may stretch back to Celtic missionary times. Certainly King David I makes reference to a great church of Linlithgow in a charter of 1138, when it was gifted to the Cathedral of St Andrews. It was dedicated, or possibly re-dedicated, by Bishop de Bernham in 1242, and consecration crosses marking where the Bishop's consecration water landed are still obvious today. The church at that time was much smaller than it is today, the less than straight south wall and the difference in style between nave and chancel indicating different building operations over the centuries. The apse was not built onto the chancel until 1531. While in architectural terms we consider St Michael's to be one of Scotland's greatest medieval churches, magnificent in splendour both inside and out, it is the church's story, its place in Scotland's history, that so fascinates us. So before we take our tour round the church, let us look at its involvement in some of the great Scottish events.

Edward I, popularly referred to in English history books as the 'Hammer of the Scots', thought it fit, first to incorporate the church in the fortifications of the nearby castle, and then to use it as a storehouse for his war supplies, which had been sent north by ship to the port of Blackness. The church suffered from English occupation and a major fire in 1424. Work on the choir was in progress as the new century arrived, and 1540 saw the church largely in the form we recognise today. The outside of the church was home to twenty stone statues of saints, and a stone crown was in position on the top of the tower.

While Mary Queen of Scots was born in the palace in 1542, there is no way of knowing if she was baptised in the church. What we can say with assurance is that the church suffered as the Reformation swept Scotland. With the exception of St Michael, who hung on with clipped wings, the stone saints were removed from their buttresses, and more than twenty altars and the font were destroyed. In the 1600s, we see the church, or certainly part of it, being used as a wood store, and then as accommodation for Edinburgh University students and staff when a plague struck the capital. If this was bad, worse was to come. Cromwell arrived in the town in 1650, stabling his horses in the nave, with the rest of the church providing quarters for his men. A few years later, post-Reformation differences dividing the local population (between those for and against the Solemn League and Covenant), St Michael's was physically partitioned into two churches by a mid-wall to appease the factions, a state which fortunately only lasted a few years. From all accounts the interior of the church now presented a fairly grim picture. Burns, visiting St Michael's in 1787, was to comment:

> What a poor pimping place of worship is a Presbyterian place of worship; dirty, narrow and squalid, stuck in the corner of old Popish grandeur.

Burns being Burns, he was not to miss the penitent's stool, on which those who were guilty of sins of the flesh – in the opinion of the kirk session – had to present themselves in view of the congregation for so many Sundays.

In 1812 the magnificent oak ceiling required to be replaced. However, because of the war with Napoleon at that time it was not possible to bring in the necessary hardwood from Africa and a plaster ceiling was put in position. (It is hard to believe now, but such was the value of bodies for sale to the medical profession in Edinburgh at that time that it was possible to hire out cages or mortsafes for the protection of new graves in the churchyard.)

Denoting its status as one of the three mother churches of the Lothians (along with St Mary's, Haddington and St Giles, Edinburgh), the town's church was adorned with a stone crown. There seems to have been consternation in the town when, in 1820, it was discovered that the crown was in an unsafe condition and had to be demolished. Replacement plans came to naught until the 1960s, when the current eye-catching anodised timber and aluminium crown of thorns was put in position. This follows the medieval tradition that each addition to a church should be in the style of the period in which the addition is made, so emphasising the church is both ancient and modern.

Before we make our tour of the church, there is one point to clarify. St Michael's is only a few yards away from the palace and was incorporated into its defences. While it was much used by the kings and queens of the day, especially the Stuarts, it was only occasionally used as the royal chapel. That was contained within the palace itself. St Michael's has always been the church of the people of Linlithgow.

Walking through the main west door of the church, there is immediate impact. One is not prepared for the length of the church, the height to its roof, the arched stone pillars, and its cathedral magnificence. Initially one feels very small in its expanse, but then, as one moves forward, taking in the woodwork, the rich red carpet in the chancel, and the feel that this is a church that is being used, it exudes a surprising coothiness for all its size and majesty. It is truly a remarkable experience.

Standing in the porch, one notices the door leading to the bell tower. The church has three bells; St Michael, Alma Maria and Meg Duncan. The last name does not sound very 'kirkie' and may raise a query. Legend has it that Meg Duncan is named after an old lady who lived near to where the Star and Garter Hostelry now stands. She had a very long tongue and on a Sunday morning would lean out of her window and in a resonant voice would shout, 'hurry up' to the folk making their way to the church. Alma Maria is one of the oldest bells in Scotland, it carries the date '1490', and bears the inscription in Latin, 'The people of Linlithgow made me'. Along from the door to the bell tower is the first of the artefacts that make a tour round St Michael's so fascinating. It is a facsimile of the National Covenant proclaiming support for the Presbyterian Church against the introduction of Episcopacy. Admittedly some of the writing is rather indistinct, but a bit of effort will show the first signature to be that of the Marquis of Montrose – soldier of brilliance, man of letters, one of the great 'Flowers of Scotland'.' How many have quoted his famous lines?

He either fears his fate too much,
Or his deserts are small,
That dares not put it to the touch,
To gain or lose it all.

In this entrance area, with its canopied benches, is a beautiful tapestry, the first you will see as you move round the church. These remarkable works of art, each telling a particular story of Linlithgow life, have been composed by members of the congregation and friends of the church. Look at the window above the entrance doors, which portrays the Transfiguration. Even on the dullest of days, there is a remarkable sparkle to be seen on and around the figure of Christ.

Turning to the right one passes an aumbry (or recessed cupboard) in the stone wall. This leads to the priests' quarters in the roof area, left from the days when St Michael's was a Catholic church. In the south west corner is a font, placed near the doorway to symbolise a child's entrance to the church through baptism. The tapestry here is particularly unusual as it depicts Mary Queen of Scots, not in her customary black, but in pink, the colour she wore on her return from France. A consecration cross can be seen on the wall. One would expect to find twelve in the church, referring, some would say, to the twelve tribes of Israel, others, to the twelve disciples. Some of these crosses are in the most unlikely of places, indicating that the walls of St Michael's have had their ups and downs over the centuries. The Lepers' Squint is worth a study. In bygone years, lepers were not allowed into the church for fear of contamination, although their right to Christian worship was recognised. The squint – a small window – allowed them to see the Mass being performed. In its Catholic era, over twenty altars to various saints were positioned around the church.

Some stonework extends out from the south wall. This reminds us that at one time there were not pews as there are today. Members of the congregation brought their own stools, or simply stood. Services could last for hours and attendance was hard on the old and infirm, so ledges were available for them to sit on – which gave rise to the expression about the weaker 'going to the wall'.

On the subject of pews there is much to say. The movement from standing to formalised seating was neither swift nor structured. Initially, as has been said, parishioners simply brought their own stools to church. Sections of the floor were allocated to the King and to various guilds, and they built seats and pews according to whim. The sartorially inclined Incorporation of Tailors went to town by building their pew higher than any other – allowing them to look down on the King – and decorating their woodwork with the symbols of their craft. The magistrates eventually decreed that all pews should be uniform, although their layout seems to have been exempted from this. We learn from a town council record of 1672 that 26 pews faced the pulpit, which was then on the south side; 19 faced the east and 10 pointed to the west. Lofts were provided for the King and magistrates, and others for the guilds, with the cordiners (or shoemakers) taking up the most space. The lofts eventually became galleries of distinction and were not removed until 1896, when the seating we have today was installed. The pulpit, we have to say, has known the odd movement or two.

Continuing our movement from the corner to the east, we pass on the right a window depicting the Four Evangelists as writers, and on the left a splendid tapestry reminding us of the trades prominent in the town. Then we arrive at the south transept, known as St Katherine's Aisle. Here, one must spend a little time. In medieval days this was a separate chapel, much used by James IV, and it is thought to have been a meeting place of the Lyon Court. The window, with its specially prepared tones using the minimum of paint, was designed by the Scottish artist Crear McCartney to commemorate the 750th anniversary of the consecration of the church. The upper part of the window portrays Pentecost,

St Katherine's Aisle, where James IV saw his vision before the Battle of Flodden

with the Tongues of Fire shooting out from the centre to reach the traditional symbols of the Apostles. Lower down in the window we find six lancets telling the story of the New Jerusalem from the Revelation of St John.

For many, the most fascinating thing about this aisle is the legend of the 'Blue Man'. To tell the story we must delve into history, to when James IV was on the throne. James, you may remember, had married Margaret, a daughter of Henry VII of England, bringing together the Thistle and the Rose. We believe it to have been a love match. But when England went to war with France, James felt bound to honour the Auld Alliance and decided to lead an army across the Border to do battle with the English. Before setting out, James attended devotions in his little chapel and, while at prayers, there appeared a vision warning him of a disaster ahead if he was intent on war. James disregarded this advice, led his army over the Border, and Scotland suffered a catastrophic defeat at Flodden. Whether James really saw a vision or not, we shall never know. The King was very superstitious; the church was dark and only lit by candles. It has often been suggested that the ghost was really a servant dressed up by Margaret, who was intent on avoiding war between her father and husband. Sir Walter Scott, in his epic tale *Marmion*, gives no guidance:

> In Katharine's aisle the monarch knelt,
> With sackcloth-shirt and iron belt,
> And eyes with sorrow streaming;

The vision appears and displays little reverence to the King:

> In a low voice, – but never tone
> So thrill'd through vein, and nerve, and bone:–
> 'My mother sent me from afar,
> Sir King, to warn thee not to war,–

Moving on, we pass a gravestone with the writing unusually arrayed round its edges. The name 'Forrest' suggests one of the first martyrs of the Reformation. Interesting to note here that burials took place within the church until 1813. In a cabinet, there is a Book of Remembrance for the use of congregational members. And a Piscina in the wall reminds us that in Catholic days wine left over after mass was drained down to the founds of the church. The tapestry in this area depicts St Celia, the patron saint of music, acknowledging the fact that the church moved with the times and installed an organ in 1877.

We are now in the Queen's Aisle, which was converted into a small chapel in 1986. It is good to be able to say that all the furnishings were built in Linlithgow by local tradesmen. One's eyes focus on the bronze casting on the east wall. Rather unusually, Linlithgow has its war memorial inside a church, and this is where wreaths are laid at armistice time. The tapestry displayed in the aisle expresses our 'Hopes for Peace'.

Entering the Chancel, one is struck by the vivid colours of the carpet and by its design, which displays the cross of St Michael, with its rounded extremities. The unbroken chain represents the Celtic symbol of eternity. Equally striking is the window in memory of Sir Wyville Thomson, which dominates the apse. We shall spend time with him and his famous sea-going *Challenger* expedition further on. The theme of the window is the Creation, based on Psalm 104, and it is a worthwhile exercise to study it with the script in hand. But if you have a child with you, be prepared to explain away the sight of a blue lobster.

The carved woodwork in the apse warrants our attention, especially on the reredos and the elders' stalls. Fruits, flowers, birds and animals – including a mouse, a squirrel, a rabbit, an otter and a frog – have been carved in this area, and it seems sad that such delightful workmanship is so far away from the congregation. Part of an old stone reredos was found when digging in the church graveyard, and this is now incorporated in the vestry wall.

The pulpit is worth viewing because of the connection it shows with the royal family, featuring carvings of four queens. Queen Margaret is recognisable by her pigtails, and worthy of her place because she made gifts to the church of lands and a hospital. Mary Queen of Scots was born in the palace and is thought to have been baptised in the church. The link with Victoria is rather tenuous. On her last visit to Linlithgow, she went straight through the town without stopping, leaving a confused provost standing hanging on to his speech of welcome. But at one point during her reign, the appointment of a minister to St Michael's needed her approval. Our present queen has always taken an active interest in the church and – as a point of interest – when worshipping in the church has not used the royal pew, but has requested a chair to be positioned in front of the congregation.

We are now walking westwards and should enter the north transept. On a wall is mounted a bead board, listing the names of all the ministers or priests in charge of St Michael's since the thirteenth century. There is a sad story connected with the little Samuel window in the transept; it was installed by Rev. John Ferguson, whose commitment to St Michael's over some 30 years was tremendous. Unfortunately, he was not a lucky man; one of his daughters burned to death in a fire in his manse, and another was drowned on the loch while skating. He installed the Samuel window, it is said, as a reminder of what life had given him and what it had taken away.

Hard right on the transept is the town pew, overlooked by a magnificent coat of arms. They are not related – the coat of arms belongs to the Duke of Cumberland. In the year 1746, both Prince Charles Edward Stuart and the Duke of Cumberland arrived in Linlithgow. Neither left with good reputations. The Prince's army behaved badly, and, later, Cumberland's troops, intentionally or not, burned down the palace. Perhaps Cumberland ended up ahead on points, as he was later made a Freeman of Linlithgow.

On the way back to the west entrance you can see the bricked up doorway that was once used by visiting monarchs. There are many marks on the church's pillars; not just masons' and sword sharpening marks, but the scores and indents left by troops quartered here, often with horses and wagons in tow. These marks encourage the thought, 'If these stones could only speak.'

CHAPTER 6

The Linlithgow Players

Linlithgow Players in Action

WE CAN IMAGINE that in the Daft Days of James IV, many actors were in attendance when the court settled in Linlithgow. What we can say with assurance is that one of our great plays was performed in Linlithgow in the sixteenth century, when James V was on the throne. His friendship with his 'Lyon King at Arms', Sir David Lyndsay, was close, and this may explain his tolerance for Lyndsay's great satire *The Three Estates*, which he presented before the King in Linlithgow. The performance of such a morality play – which takes the King, church and people to task – would, without doubt, have been forbidden in England or on the continent.

The Linlithgow Players as we know them today were formed in 1943. They are an important part of town life, bringing enjoyment both to locals and to visitors to the town. Apart from one short break, the Players have been producing plays, tableaux and pantomimes since their inception.

The Spring Production is probably the *raison d'être* for the players – a conventional play with a full set, performed at the Linlithgow Academy Theatre. It is an opportunity for serious actors to get to grips with dramatic roles and study the craft of theatre at length and in depth. Over the years, the Players have mounted productions of plays by Ayckbourn, Ibsen, Priestley and Rattigan. Nor have Scottish plays been neglected, and many will remember the enjoyment obtained from attending such as the *Flowers of Edinburgh*. The Players have staged *Macbeth* in St Michael's Church, *A Midsummer Night's Dream* in the Rose Garden, plays about Mary Queen of Scots in the Great Hall of the palace, and one about miners in Laetare International Centre. Their triumphant 2005 production of Neil Simon's *Plaza Suite* was presented to the people of Bo'ness at their Barony Theatre.

Undoubtedly one of the Players' most popular productions is their traditional pantomime in January. For over ten years, the Central Scotland Ballet School has helped with the dancing, and occasional guests have included the Town Crier, the Reed Band and the Rugby Club Choir. The panto involves a lot of hard work by all branches of the Players – actors, wardrobe, stage crew, lighting and sound. Planning usually starts in February, when they choose the title of the next production. The Players have been very fortunate in having their pantos written by their own members, first by the late Bob Martin and now by Peter Anderson, a published author and playwright. A large cast is needed for a big, bright panto, so extra actors, both adult and children, are invited to swell the Players' numbers. November and December are spent in rehearsal. Then, Christmas and New Year over, another Players Panto Production is welcomed in the town.

On August Sundays, under the auspices of Historic Scotland, the palace is used as a backdrop for the Linlithgow Players' historical re-enactments, with the object of presenting painlessly the history of the palace to the public. The oldest production depicting the return of Mary Stuart to Linlithgow was written by the late Bob Martin; a visit to the court of James v is the most recent and was written by Peter Anderson. The Players are a very versatile bunch and the same actor or actress may play different roles each week, depending on who is available.

In the autumn the Players present a 'Plays and Wine' evening, which involves a selection of one act plays. It is an ideal opportunity for new actors, playwrights or directors to practice their craft under the eye of a more experienced Player. There is a chance to produce plays for the Scottish Community Drama Association (SCDA) One-Act Play Competition, and on no fewer than five occasions over recent years the Players have won the SCDA Lothian District One-Act Play Competition.

There are other occasional items in the Players' Calendar. For instance, in

2004 the National Archives of Scotland commissioned the Players to record the soundtrack for a set of historical CDs to supplement History lessons for Scottish youngsters. In 2003, the Players presented a son et lumière at Linlithgow Palace, written, produced and directed on behalf of Historic Scotland. Although every drama group needs actors, there is also a lot of work to be done behind the scenes; the Players' teams of costume makers, set builders and sound and lighting technicians reach very high standards and offer their services to other organisations in the town.

In addition to the Players normal enactments in the Palace in July and August, September 2006 will see a new enactment from the Players as they seek to commemorate the Battle of Linlithgow Bidge which took place in 1526. It promises to be the kind of local history they present so well. James V had been born in the Palace in 1512 and was only a year old when his father was killed at Flodden. For the next sixteen years such great nobles as the Red Douglas, Earl of Lennox, various Hamiltons, Scott of Buccleugh, the Earl of Glencairn would plot and fight to have control over the young king, the most bloody occasion being the Battle of Linlithgow Bridge. The viaduct of the Edinburgh-Glasgow rail line crosses the battlefield and there is, of course, the roadside cairn on the way to the leisure centre which is said to mark the spot where Lennox, having surrendered to the Laird of Pardovan, was murdered by Sir James Hamilton. The Players' approach to this enactment is to view the battle through the eyes of some non-combatants. It is an imaginative approach.

The last weekend of October 2006 saw, with a view to celebrating life in the town, the holding of a new Arts Weekend when many organisations offered entertainment and the Players presented a Scots play. Looking further ahead, Peter Anderson has again been working with pen in hand on his next panto. It is to be the 'Sleeping Beauty'.

CHAPTER 7

The Deacons Court and Marches Day

Up townsmen, up! And hail the gladsome morning
The sun o'er Binny Craig has ope'd his knuckle e'e,
Our auld burgh town wi' his glorious light adorning,
Welcome! O welcome, the merry Marches day.

QUEEN ANNE IS supposed to have had Calais inscribed on her heart. Such is the enthusiasm of many in the town, Black Bitches and incomers alike, for the Riding of the Marches, that one often suspects their cardiac organs bear the town's motto. The traditional day of the Marches, the first Tuesday after the second Thursday in June, is for many a day comparable in importance with such other calendar days as Christmas and their birthdays. It is a day when hair gets let down, the town's strong community spirit is worn on the sleeve, and expats return to greet old friends. It is a happy day.

One hopes not to see the friction today that often occurred at the Marches in days gone by. William Hutton in his tale *Simon Moneypenny* tells how Marches Day was regarded, along with St Magdalene Fair Day, as a day for the physical settling of grievances. George Waldie in his 1858 history of the town gives an insight into the end of day proceedings:

The proceedings of the day are usually wound up with a dinner. When each Incorporation had its own dinner, and manners were somewhat rougher, talk would be of 'former days' similar to this, on which bailies were unhors'd, standards broke, their bearers thrown in the mire; how the blood stream'd alternately from the sides of wayward horse and the skulls of wayward riders; how magistrates were assaulted, councillors batter'd, and deacons trampled under foot.

Memories were either short in these times or the Town Clerk was not taken seriously as he proclaimed at the 'Fencing of the Marches':

I Defend and I Forbid in our Soverign Lady's name, and in the name of My Lord Provost and Baillies of the Royal Burgh of Linlithgow, That no person or persons presume nor take upon hand, under whatever colour or pretex, to trouble or molest the Magistrates and Burgesses in their peaceable riding of the town's, Marches under all highest pains and charges that after may follow. – God Save the Queen.

We cannot be positive about the date of the first Riding of the Marches. Linlithgow was acknowledged as a Burgh in 1389. A Minute of Council dated 19 October 1541, when James V was on the throne, confirms a Riding of the Marches took place in that year. As it does not suggest this was a first Riding, it is reasonable to suppose the Marches were ridden before that date. The town's boundaries were, after all, of importance to those both within and without them. We learn that around this time the town's hangman led the Marches procession. And we believe representatives of the town attended the Ridings of other burghs, as they were still largely free from outside pressure at this time, and unity meant the strength to allow that freedom to continue. Early Ridings were done by a small party of officials and men of importance in the town, but as the procession became more significant and formalised the various guilds and fraternities – with their banners streaming behind them – were included in the events of the day. In times gone by, as is the case today, the boundaries examined were Linlithgow Bridge and Blackness. No walking appears to have been done to the north or south of the town outwith the town wall. And we note that having enjoyed a refreshment at the Bridge and returned to the town, there was an element of haste to get to Blackness, as Cockwell in his soliloquy describes:

> Weel faith this is ae dayo' the year, on which ev'ry body pits on their best; and I'm resolv'd to show't as weel's I can. Whan I munt my horse, I'll gi' him the spur, gallop to the deec'ns , and daz the ane shall gang in the ranks afore me; and as we gang east to the Cross, I'll glee to this side and that side, kepp the lasses een, and smile in their faces, gar my horse carry a high head, keep my taes into his side, and caper away fu' bonnily: – and then down at Blackness – O I'll get rair fun!

In 1834 the then-Provost, one Adam Dawson, decided that at the Marches the Provost and magistrates should lead the procession instead of bringing up the rear. Being a man of ideas (or opposed to exercise), he also instituted the Riding in carriages.

Change is inevitable and in 1974 Linlithgow town council moved into the history books as local government reorganisation took place. The old council had organised the Marches, but they had become so much a part of town life they could not be allowed to depart the scene. It is interesting to extract a quote from Waldie's *History of Linlithgow* here – was ever a local historian more wrong?

> The ceremony as already seen is an old one, and it appears in its origin to have been something more than a mere ceremony. Since the dissolutions of the Incorporations, it has been gradually dying away, and threatens at no distant period to become extinct.

The town's answer to reorganisation – and the answer of Dr Bill Wilson, the last elected Provost – was to institute the Court of the Deacons of the Ancient and Royal Burgh of Linlithgow, with responsibility for continuing the tradition and raising such funds as would be necessary. It was a brave and popular decision. The chairman of the Court would be known as the Provost and the senior elected members as Baillies. On Marches Day and special occasions the ermine trimmed red robes of old would be worn, as would the Provost's chain of office.

The world moves on and today – with the exception of the Dyers, who turn out immaculately in morning dress – there is little link to be seen with the old trades of the town. However, the various clubs and charities in the town have taken over from the historic fraternities, and they present their Deacons at the two Deacons Nights which are forerunners of the Marches Day itself.

The bands can still be heard early on Marches Day. The day begins with the Provost's grand breakfast – invitations to this sumptuous affair are prized. He and his guests fraternise with the Dyers and other organisations at the palace. They award prizes to the best floats, then, at 11am, the procession (accompanied by the sound of bells) makes for 'the Brig', the local name for Linlithgow Bridge. Refreshment is given, a speech or two is made, and everybody returns to town. The floats are put away. At this point there is a notable hurry, as Blackness is in the sights. There – at the old port of Linlithgow – the Baron Baillie welcomes everyone, toasts of Blackness Milk are enjoyed, and the Fencing of the Court takes place on the Green of Blackness (adjoining the site of St Ninian's Chapel). The Baron Baillie is appointed for the next year (the present incumbent, Bobby Fleming, follows in the footsteps of his father and grandfather). A late lunch is eaten (it is usually somewhat on the noisy side), there is more fraternising, then everyone gets in position for the grand procession from the Low Port at five o'clock. To the cheers of the citizens, the procession, with all the bands playing different tunes, makes its traditional perambulation three times round the Cross. The Provost and Deacons mount the stairs to the Burgh Halls, and following a speech from 'My Lord of the Dyers' the Provost reports the town's boundaries are intact and ends with the words, 'Safe out, Safe in'. 'Auld Lang Syne' brings an end to ceremony.

Some years ago the Deacons Court issued a booklet, *Linlithgow Marches*. It is recommended reading for those who would like to know more about that 'first Tuesday after the second Thursday in June every year'.

As an indication of how the procession would once have been made up, the following list gives guidance:

Bo'ness & Carriden Band
Carriages with four horses with Provost and magistrates
Constabulary
Carriage with two horses with Treasurer, Dean of Guild, Town Clerk and Fiscal
Carriages with councillors and guests
Incorporation of Hammermen
Incorporation of Baxters
Bathgate Band
Incorporation of Cordiners and Linlithgow Natives Edinburgh Association
Incorporation of Wrights
Masons and Bricklayers
Fraternity of Tanners
Fraternity of Whipmen
Fraternity of Curriers
Painters
Pipe Band
Distillery employees
Lochmill paperworkers
Candlemakers
Miners
Good Templars
Cricketers
Football club
Other societies as fixed by the Marshal
Broxburn Band
Fraternity of Dyers
Private carriages
Marshall of Marches – Deputy Chief Constable

To those who query the importance of such traditions as the Marches, it is worth pondering over the words of John Buchan (Lord Tweedsmuir), speaking as Warden of Neidpath Castle at the Beltane Festival of Peebles in 1935:

I do not believe you can exaggerate the importance of the preservation of old ways and customs, and all these little things that bind a man to his place. Today we live in difficult times. The steamroller of progress is flattening out many of our old institutions, and there is a danger of a general decline in idiom and distinctive quality in our Scottish life. The only way to counteract this peril is to preserve jealously all these elder things which are bone of our bone and flesh of our flesh. For remember, no man can face the future with courage and confidence unless it is solidly founded on the past. And conversely, no problem will be too hard, no situation too strange if we can link it with what we know and love.

Any comment on the Marches must include that elegant body of men, The Fraternity of Dyers. With their motto, 'We Dye to Live – We Live to Dye', the Fraternity claims to be a pioneer of Friendly Societies in Scotland. Certainly their roots go back a long way. With a long involvement with the Marches, their Deacons have been recorded back to 1713. A Minute book of that year is still in existence. But reference to dyers and dying can be traced back to the early 1600s and it is reasonable to assume an early link with 'fullers', who would compact cloth by shrinking and beating. Certainly there is an absence of records of the Incorporation of Cloth Walkers or Fullers after 1646, which suggests some form of amalgamation with the dyers had taken place.

The dyers have given proud and often generous service to the town. Long may they continue to occupy their distinguished position at the rear of the procession.

CHAPTER 8

Children's Gala Day

FESTIVALS OF VARIOUS forms and origins can be found the breadth and length of Scotland. Some – like the Beltane ceremony in Peebles – are Celtic in origin. Others have their roots in the feast day of a saint. Their religious aspects may have died with the Reformation, but the festivals survive in a modern form. It is said the Bo'ness Fair has its origins in 1774, when a law was passed freeing miners from servitude. Herring Queen festivals celebrating the return of the fishing fleet to port are held in places as far apart as Wick and Eyemouth. In Central Scotland, gala days are generally associated with the mining industry, although in West Lothian their roots often lie with Friendly Society events or even just sports days.

The Linlithgow & Linlithgow Bridge Children's Gala came to life in 1920. There have been certain changes in its structure over the years but essentially it is a day for children and – as it now takes place on the Saturday following the Marches – it is regarded as part of the town's civic celebrations, and enjoys great popularity.

The gala day centres round the crowning of the Gala Queen, with well over a 100 children attached to the Queen's retinue. Letters are sent to all the pupils in local primary schools asking if they want to take part in the coming gala. The previous year's Queen pulls names out of a hat to decide who gets what role, with the position of Queen Elect being confined to Primary 7 applicants. Whether the Queen is selected from their ranks or not, every local primary school brings their own float to the parade. No less than seven rehearsals are held.

The evening before the gala day, a band plays outside the home of the Queen Elect. There is quite a mustering job to be done on the morning of the gala. There are 20 children in the main retinue, supported by 40 fairies, 50 flower girls, around 14 bower girls and the same number of guards. Local halls are used as gathering points and a marquee is erected in Justinhaugh Drive for the guests. These will be local figures, teachers, representatives from other galas, some invited senior citizens and, of course, the main speaker of the afternoon. At midday, the procession sets off.

It is a long procession – up to eight bands play – and can take over half an hour to pass any given point. Floats, decorated bicycles, carriages, and many youth organisations merge with bower and flower girls, fairies and kilted guards.

On arrival at the Peel, all eyes turn to the specially erected stage, where the Dowager Queen steps down. Then the big moment arrives and the new Queen is crowned. A programme of entertainment follows, and the main speaker is heard. The Queen's first official visit is to St Michael's Hospital and Linlithgow's sheltered housing, where she speaks to the various residents. She lays a wreath at the war memorial in St Michael's Church. Later there is a meal in the Burgh Hall and the Queen addresses the town.

Bowers play an important part in gala day celebrations. West Lothian and Falkirk press reports of the 1850s make mention of their being constructed with spruce and laurel and decorated with flowers of the season. As gala day approaches in Linlithgow, many streets look like builders' yards, as fathers and friends vie with one another to build the best edifice from which their offspring can depart for the gala.

CHAPTER 9

The Major Recreational Clubs of Linlithgow

Linlithgow Rose Football Club

LINLITHGOW ROSE F.C.
Real Estate Signs Ltd 01506 847766

WINNERS OF:

OVD Junior Cup
League Champions
League Cup

St.Michael's Cup
Brown Cup
Fife & Lothians Cup

Main Sponsor   Tel: 01506 842881
R McNicoll Car & Van Hire

LINLITHGOW ROSE FOOTBALL CLUB is regarded affectionately in its home town. It boasts one of the finest junior football grounds in Scotland. Although there are mentions of junior football being played in Linlithgow at an earlier date, we are concerned here with the group who had the enthusiasm and courage to form the club in 1889. A pitch was obtained in Captain's Park near Boghall and, after the holding of fund raising events, strips were purchased. Not in the familiar maroon of today, but black and white, colours which still served as the club's second strip until a few years ago.

Linlithgow had to wait thirteen years before it had a football trophy to celebrate. In 1902 the crowds cheered as the local band played the team round the town, when they returned as winners of the Forth League (they had beaten Inverkeithing Thistle in the final at Tynecastle). Two years later, the Rose won the County Cup, and in the 1909/10 and 1910/11 seasons they won the St Michael's Cup, now known as the MRS Cup. The club then moved from the Captain's Park to Upper Mains Park, where, by defeating Portobello Thistle, they won the

Lumley Cup. The two teams were to meet in another final ten years later, when Portobello took their revenge.

In 1924 there was a structural change in the Association, with all the county teams coming together to form the West Lothian Junior League. Rose became the first league champions. There followed considerable success. In the next year, the team won the Thornton Shield and the County Cup, and in 1926/27 the St Michael's Cup, Brown Cup and the County Cup. In 1930 there was another change of pitch as playing moved to the Lower Mains Park. To handsel the new ground in style, the team beat Bonnyrigg Athletic 9–1.

There are some footballers who, due to a combination of their skills and their qualities as a person, achieve a revered status. Tommy Walker was of that mould, and as a schoolboy he was signed by the Rose (after a long tussle with his father) for the sum of three pounds and two shillings. Indeed, such was the enthusiasm to sign him that the secretary of the time, Alex Wood, in company with Tommy Ure, walked all the way to Livingston and back on more than one occasion to discuss arrangements with Walker's parents. (Alex Wood, incidentally, was the grandfather of the late *Gazette* journalist Vic Wood, while Tommy Ure's namesake grandson played for the Rose for 14 years.) A year later, Linlithgow Rose was 35 pounds better off as Tommy Walker transferred to Heart of Midlothian FC. Walker continued at Hearts for many years, serving as player, manager and a director. He was capped for Scotland, had a spell with Chelsea, but perhaps above all, was seen as a role model for young people, representing all that is good in sport. When the Rose won the Scottish Junior Cup in 1965, Walker was there to see their victory, and to hand a bottle of wine into the dressing room.

The Rose did not win any honours during the 1930s, and had an uncomfortable time financially. On one occasion a new player had to accept an IOU, as the committee men charged with the signing didn't have enough money to pay him. Problems also arose with the new owners of Mains Park, who – while giving the club assurances they could continue to play at the site – indicated their intention to build a greyhound stadium there. Then war was declared. Equipment was tucked away safely, debts were paid, and twenty pounds was lodged in the bank. The Rose closed down for the duration of hostilities.

After the war, the club had to be built again from scratch. A very dedicated committee, under President A.C. Ford, started fund raising in earnest, and searched for suitable land to play at. Nevertheless, it was not until the end of January 1947 that the desired ground – in Braehead Road – was obtained. Various names were considered for the new purchase, and Preston was selected. Two years later it was changed to the name we know today – Prestonfield. The ground had to be knocked into shape before it could be used, and an army of volunteers started work. On 5 August 1949, the Rose played their first home competitive match for ten years. Their opponents were Broxburn Athletic, and three thousand turned up to watch the game.

The newly reformed Rose won the East of Scotland Cup in the 1953/54 season with a victory over Fauldhouse United, and a few weeks later they defeated Broxburn Athletic to add the Thornton Shield to the cabinet. The next ten years were not to see any awards come to Prestonfield, but with perseverance all was to change – and to change quite dramatically.

At the start of the 1964/65 season, the funds totalled less than a £100. The transfer of a player, a garden fête, and the sale of some scrap metal stabilised the position. Then old rivals Bo'ness United were beaten 3–1. This started an amazing run of 39 games without defeat. On 15 May 1965, at Hampden Park, 35,500 people saw Linlithgow Rose win the Scottish Junior Cup, defeating Baillieston Juniors by three goals to one. That famous Rose side should be recorded: McGlynn, Reston, Syme, Veitch, Grant, Gardner, Henderson, Grant, Cowie, Fordyce and Oliphant. To the Scottish Cup, the Rose added the Edinburgh District League Championship, Brown Cup, Lanark and Lothian Cup and East of Scotland Cup. The celebrations on the team's return from Hampden went on all night. After they had been led the length of the town in an open top bus by the Reed and Pipe Bands, they were greeted by Provost Baird on the steps of the Town Hall. A civic reception followed. What is absolutely remarkable is that the season's success was achieved with a playing staff of only thirteen.

The Rose were now at the forefront of Junior football in Scotland. In 1968, the club reached the semi-finals of the Scottish Junior Cup, and in 1974 lost the final 3–1 to Cambuslang Rangers. In the 25 years following their success at Hampden, a further 39 trophies came to Prestonfield.

Shortly after winning the Scottish Junior Cup, thought was given to the building of a social club to act as a focus point for supporters of the team. The usual problems – finding suitable ground with adequate parking; obtaining planning permission – were encountered, and it was not until 1971 that a brewery offered a suitable package, which was accepted. Progress thereafter was at speed, and the social club opened officially in November 1973. Membership was in great demand and soon reached the 1,400 mark. Extensions and improvements have gone ahead over the years, and the club has provided finance to improve facilities at Prestonfield in general.

The early years of the millennium were good to the Rose. At Partick Thistle's ground in 2002, they won the Scottish Junior Cup by defeating Auchinleck

Talbot 1–0. The Deacons Court provided a civic reception. But, while hopes were high for a repeat performance the next year, the fates were not kind, and the Rose were defeated by Tayport in the final. However, 2002 also saw the erection of the splendid new stand at Prestonfield. Bearing in mind that only a tiny handful of the 166 junior football clubs in Scotland have stands, the structure is a testimony to the commitment of the members of the Rose. Because of the amenities it now offers, including floodlighting, Prestonfield has hosted international matches, and both Rangers and Livingston have made use of the ground for reserve team matches. The stand bears the name of Davie Roy, and it is a well deserved honour.

Davie Roy MBE, Secretary of Linlithgow Rose

Davie Roy started with Polkemmet Juniors and played for several local sides. A broken leg did not help his playing career, and he took up a coach/manager position with Avon Star, an under 21 side at Linlithgow Bridge. A year later, in 1959, he accepted an invitation to join the Rose as its secretary, and he has been an outstanding success. He served as President of the East of Scotland Association 1969–72, as Vice President of the Scottish Junior Football Association 1974–76, and as the Association President 1976–81. In these latter capacities he also served as a member of the Scottish Football Association. In 1999 he was awarded an MBE for Services to Junior football.

An honours board is positioned at the entrance to the social club of Linlithgow Rose. Only a quick glance at the board is needed to realise the standing the club has in the world of Junior football. Thirty members of the club have achieved international status, two of them – John Binnie and Bobby Kirk – as managers. Since its return to football after the war years, Linlithgow Rose has, in addition to its national wins, won the following:

East of Scotland Cup – 12 times
East of Scotland League – 13 times
Fife and Lothian Cup – 12 times
St Michael's Cup – 10 times

Linlithgow Rugby Football Club

Considering the current total commitment of players to the game, and today's emphasis on fitness, it brings a smile to the face to recall the smoky atmosphere in the Star and Garter the night the club was officially formed. Talks had been going on in dribs and drabs about forming a rugby club for some months. The Cricket Club was anxious to obtain an income during the winter months through the sharing of bar premises. Everything came together that night in the Star and Garter. A club would be formed which would rent the Cricket Club facilities at Boghall. The colours would be red and black, and sufficient beer would be consumed in the Cricket Club bar to ensure the rent could be paid, and that the Rugby Club's overheads could be satisfied. It was, to put it mildly, a leap into the dark. Financially, for quite a while, life would not be easy.

The new club (one had existed in the 1920s for a few years) did not lack enthusiasm and, young as the players were, it was obvious that there was talent in the ranks, and good talent at that. But there was a shortage of experience and guile and some of the non-Linlithgow club players in the town, who carried their boots to their Edinburgh clubs on a Saturday, could have made a tremendous contribution to the fledgling club. But the next season saw an increased membership, a marked improvement in the quality of play and an emphasis on establishing a good social life to discourage potential players from casting their eyes at the fashionable clubs twenty miles to the east. Those who lived through those early social evenings at Boghall will not forget them. The camaraderie was intense.

And so the club moved forward. The club's first captain, John Cotton, was a splendid choice. A more than useful player, John had the sort of personality that people warm to, and it was a measure of the team's progress that when his former club of Prescot, Lancashire, came to play at Linlithgow, they went down 26–0. There was delight at the end of the season when the news was received that the club had been accepted into Division Three of the Edinburgh district league. The bad news was that the Cricket Club was concerned at the damage rugby was doing to their ground. It was time to find another pitch.

Few rugby teams warrant a mention in Hansard, but Linlithgow managed it. A request to use the Peel having been turned down in a perfunctory style, the support of Tam Dalyell MP was requested and given. The battle was not to be confined to the locality, where there was already vigorous discussion, but reached the House of Commons – before the then Secretary of State turned down the request. But the truth of the advice 'it pays to advertise' was proven when a *Gazette* advert resulted in the offer of a field from Mr Gardiner of Springfield. This was gratefully accepted, though it entailed the unusual chore of moving cattle from the pitch before a game. Unfortunately, the cattle were not house trained, and a few scintillating conversations took place, with visiting clubs holding that 'the Reds', as they were now known, had a moral obligation to pay for the laundering of their strips. But when Provost Fergus Byrne made a statement that the rugby club was an asset to the town, he gave a hint that a future home at Mains Park was a possibility.

When Bill Campbell and Colin Wells succumbed to the blandishments of Gerry Keating and joined the club, their impact was phenomenal, and it was not surprising that 1974 ended with the Reds at the top of their division, and Colin being selected for the district. Bill later received district honours. And when Craig Loudoun donned the red jersey, the club had one of its all time great packs. This is not to imply that the backs were inferior – they too were brimful of talent. With Dougie McNish as coach and the late and much loved Mike Williams as President, and with three teams frequently playing, there was a general feeling of confidence for the future.

The first club dinner was held in 1977, when membership hit the 200 mark. The club appeared on the Murrayfield international pitch in 1979, as it reached the final of the Murrayfield Cup against Portobello. Recording wins over Falkirk, Corstorphine, Ross High and Murrayfield on the way, this was a magnificent achievement.

The decade that started in 1980 saw the club achieve much playing distinction, but the most important single event was unquestionably the obtaining of pitches and the building of a clubhouse at Mains Park. After years of wandering and living an unsettled existence, the club was able to put down roots and become an integral part of Linlithgow life. In 1981, a lease was obtained from West Lothian district council, allowing a clubhouse and appropriate facilities to be built adjacent to a newly created pitch on reclaimed land. There was little delay in making use of the pitch and David Cook, the then Provost of the town, officially kicked off the first Mains Park game on 12 September 1981. But much hard work lay ahead in designing and constructing the clubhouse. Indeed it was more than hard work; it was a very considerable learning experience, and brought worry and grey hairs as many members sought to maintain professional standards in the demanding new venture, while also carrying on their normal day jobs. The commitment of five development teams over a three year period should never be forgotten. These teams were:

Design, led by Craig Loudon; Finance, led by Jim MacIntyre; Legal, led by the late Fraser Morrison; Constitution, led by John Cotton; Sponsorship, led by Bob Couser.

On 30 March 1983, there was great celebration as a Presidents XV played a Cooptomists XV, with George Thomson, the President of the Scottish Rugby Union, performing the official inauguration ceremony.

Many improvements have been made to the clubhouse over the years, but comment must be made on one very fine bit of ornamentation. The club possesses a quite remarkable collection of jerseys from national teams and a variety of others. Most were presented with the donor's good wishes, some through a bit of arm twisting, and at least two because of one Irish-man's charm and ruthless refusal to accept a 'no'. On show too is the

A Section of the Jersey Showcase at the Rugby Club

jersey of Andy Leslie, the All Blacks captain, whose father emigrated from Linlithgow. In due course Andy Leslie would visit the club and be made a life member. And thanks to Dr Ken McKenzie, who accompanied the Scottish squad to Australia in 1992, the jersey of the then Australian captain, Nick Farr-Jones, is also displayed.

One could describe the playing in the eighties in glowing terms and many see it as the heyday of the club. The winning of the Murrayfield Cup in 1981 was a tremendous achievement, and the club returned to Murrayfield the next year to reach the semi-finals of the Sevens Tournament. The Almond Quaich was collected the next year at Livingston and the Club went on to become Division Seven Champions. Once again the final of the Murrayfield Cup was reached and there was no disgrace in going down by two points to Stirling County. 1984 saw the winning of the Gowans Cup and the Sevens Tournaments of Edinburgh Northern and Hillfoots. Sevens success continued as the next season started with winning the Livingston Tournament and finished with the winning of the Murrayfield Shield, the reaching again of the Murrayfield Cup finals, and the winning of Edinburgh Northern Sevens. With admission to Division Five now achieved, there was tremendous confidence in the club. It was not a misplaced confidence, but it was an up and down season. Old hands Ronnie Hastie and Tony Oliver were regularly mentioned in press reports; Dave Turner, that most dependable of front row men, notched up his 250th appearance in the Club xv; and Jon Blundell, later to receive district honours, scored prolifically throughout the season.

The club had a year to wait until the Division Five Championship came to Mains Park. Keeping it company were the winning of the Lismore Sevens and the Gowans Cup. Against the fourth division clubs in 1988/89, Linlithgow did well and finished with a reasonable position in the league. In 1989, to reflect the increasing membership, the '200 draw' became the '300 club draw'. With a current membership of around 440, one wonders if another change of name is imminent.

One of the great joys of rugby is the meeting with and playing against teams from other countries, especially if there is the added bonus of an international match to attend. Pontyates in Wales has provided the club's longest running association, with twin town Guyancourt in second place. But other teams from Wales and France have been encountered, and games will be remembered against Irish and English and even American and Japanese sides. And in the nineties it was to become fashionable for small parties with accredited cronies to pursue the oval ball to some of its more exotic venues. The Hong Kong Sevens came first on the travellers' list, to be followed by the World Cup in South Africa and various Lions tours. In 1993, members of the club acted in various capacities in connection with the first ever World Cup Sevens Tournament, which was held at Murrayfield.

The early years of the nineties were not particularly auspicious for the first xv. On the credit side, Ian Morrison became a regular in the Scottish international squad, the clubhouse was extended, posts were erected at Lower Mains Park, and some women could be seen learning the basics of rugby. An important event was the formation of the Rugby Club Choir, which, under Jo Lavery, conductor of the Reed Band, has achieved local prominence and given much pleasure both within and outwith the town. In 2004, the choir had the experience of travelling to China to perform a series of concerts in and around Beijing.

The 1995/96 season started with Linlithgow in the third division of the restructured National Leagues. Then followed a few years of bumping up and down the division ladder. Promotion to the second division was achieved in the 1996/97 season, followed by a season in Division One. Sadly this success could not be maintained, and the club today holds its position in the second division.

In 1999, Linlithgow reached the finals of the Murrayfield Bowl, going out to Murrayfield Wanderers. A number of notable results have been achieved in the Scottish Cup, and encounters with such clubs as Boroughmuir, Melrose and Heriots have been valuable experiences. Linlithgow's totally unexpected victory over Stirling County in the third round of the Scottish Cup in 2001 should never be forgotten.

One of the great changes in the game over recent years has been in the movements of players. In both 2002 and 2003, the club sent two young players out to New Zealand to gain experience in the Land of the Long White Cloud (one of the boys, Sandy Warnock, now plays for Glasgow Hawks and is in the Scottish Under 19 squad). Such activities are obviously expensive and the club is grateful to local businesses, such as Oliphants the Bakers, for the help they give in this respect. 1997 saw the arrival of a South African, and every year the club brings over two New Zealanders to play. In their early 20s, they bring with them useful experience. One such player has gone on to play for Leicester Tigers and represented Tonga in the World Cup in Australia. Again, such importation is a costly exercise and emphasises the importance of sponsorship in today's world. On a different tack, one mentions the pride that was felt in the club when member, player, coach and district man Gordon Dixon became president of the Scottish Rugby Union in 2004/5.

All the focus has been on the first xv. But the contribution of the other teams, of which there have been many, must never be forgotten. They add much to the game and to the club. Linlithgow has always taken the development of young players seriously, and this is a policy which has proved and continues to prove to be wise.

In 1981, the decision was taken to form a mini-section for youngsters in the primary 4 to 7 range. Twenty boys turned up on the first practice Saturday to be coached by parents and former players. Now over a hundred attend for training, and games are played against other youth clubs in the Edinburgh area. One former 'mini-girl', Lee Frickelton, now plays in the Scottish Women's xv.

In 1987 there was a teachers' strike, and after the dispute was resolved there were certain difficulties in many parts of the country in getting teachers to resume sports coaching on Saturdays. Concern was expressed by many clubs that 'feeding' from school to rugby would be impaired. The answer in Linlithgow was to form a 'midi', catering for pupils at secondary schools, which was organised by Bert Lawson, Jim Lindsay and George Threadgall. Again, it has been a story of expansion. From the four boys who turned up for the first practice, the 'midi' section now has enough players to put six teams on the park, with coaching being carried out by former players, parents and a school teacher. This system, where club and school work together, has been widely adopted. Opportunities exist for 'midi' players to play against other sides, and the club has arranged playing visits, including three to Guyancourt. An annual dinner is held, with a current internationalist as the guest speaker. Overall it is a splendid approach to guiding young people into the game in general and the club in particular.

The year 2006 gave tangible evidence of the support given to the club by all ages. Over forty members showed little fear of gales as they crossed the North Sea to support 'The Peelers', the over thirty-five years section of the club as they, with three wins to their credit, won an International competition for that age group. Worthy of a mention too is the P4 mini-rugby section which became the first non-Border side to win the Galashiels mini-rugby tournament for that class.

West Lothian County Cricket Association

Cricket may be played in Linlithgow, but the reader will notice the absence of the town's name should he or she make for the pavilion that occupies the corner of the tidily grassed area known as the Boghall cricket ground. A cricket ground known as well as any in Scotland, and one with its share of success and failure, drama and excitement. There was a Linlithgow Club at one time, indeed there was more than one. In the 1880s and 90s, one of them, Linlithgow County (the county was not known as West Lothian but Linlithgowshire in those far off days) frequently boasted wins over the best sides in Scotland. In 1891, the club went through the season undefeated. The Peel provided the playing area and as many as four cricket matches might be played there on a Saturday afternoon. One wonders how many balls finished up in the loch.

However, as the 1920s progressed there seems to have been a grass roots movement which suggested it was time to raise the status of the game in the county.

The concept that grew was that of a county side fed by the small local clubs, a side which could compete against the major independent clubs and in the Scottish Counties Association. Eventually a meeting was called and on 22 August 1928, representatives of Linlithgow, Bo'ness, Fauldhouse Victoria, Philpstoun, Bathgate and Muirhouses Cricket Clubs met in the Masonic Hall in Linlithgow. With enthusiasm it was decided to form the West Lothian County Cricket Association. The news was greeted with equal enthusiasm by the press, and not only by the *Gazette*; Edinburgh and national papers endorsed the decision. The Earl of Roseberry accepted the invitation to become Honorary President, and correspondence indicates that the Counties Association agreed friendlies could be played against county sides in 1929. Provided suitable ground and a pavilion were obtained, the newcomer would be welcomed into the Counties Championship in 1930. The search for ground started.

Life has its problems at times. Negotiations started for an area of ground at Bathgate and the important and fruitful decision was taken to appoint Charles Benham as a player coach who would also supervise the necessary laying out. Refilling and excavation started. Then came the bombshell. A mining concern advised they were to extract coal from underneath the proposed ground and would not be responsible for any subsidence which occurred. Acting on advice, the new association decided not to proceed at Bathgate. To the rescue came Mr A. F. Gardiner of Springfield Farm and a lease was obtained of ground at Boghall. 1929 saw the West Lothian Association on its way, winning the first match it played against Stirling County. That first season of friendlies saw West Lothian play on a range of local club grounds including the Peel, finishing up with three wins, five defeats and nine draws. First mention here should be made of the Ford family, who have made their name so prominent in the sporting field in Linlithgow. Aleck Ford, who was capped twice while playing for Uddingston had made the first century on the Peel the year before while playing for Linlithgow.

All attention was focussed on West Lothian as it made its debut in the Scottish Counties Championship in 1930. While they finished – not unexpectedly – at the foot of the table, there had been many sparkling performances. Captain Duncan McLaren scored 102 not out including 13 fours at Alloa, and when Clackmannan County came to Boghall Aleck Ford recorded a hat trick, while at Perth they were welcomed by a crowd of a thousand.

West Lothian made its mark in 1931. Particularly satisfying were wins over such major clubs as Forfarshire and Perthshire. Professional Charlie Benham's son, Fred, joined West Lothian and so commenced a career of absolute devotion to the club. As opening bat and occasional bowler and wicketkeeper, he scored over 10,000 runs for West Lothian, with 4 centuries and 45 fifties, and made an international appearance in 1949.

1932 was a highly successful season, West Lothian, in only its fourth season in Scottish cricket, finishing second place in the Counties Championship. In 1933, West Lothian finished up third behind Fife and Perthshire. The next two years seem to have been rather shaky ones for the club. But brighter days would return and in 1936 in the Counties Championship West Lothian finished second to Fife.

Perhaps a veil should be drawn over the first match of the next year, when Heriot's FP returned the county to the dressing room with 12 runs on the board. However, Sandy Paris now found special form. After taking 7 for 49 against Perthshire, and putting the ball through the Forfarshire dressing room window, he gained his first cap for Scotland. West Lothian too would return to form and once again finished second to Fife.

The war years were obviously difficult for all cricket clubs, with so many players serving in the armed forces. The Counties Championship went into abeyance, although the Scottish Cricket Union asked clubs to maintain their fixture lists as far as possible. Of very considerable help was Mr Gardiner of Springfield's offer of a Feu Charter of the Boghall ground, for the nominal figure of one shilling. But the teams that took the field during the war years were made up of a few of the old brigade and a clutch of young people, most of them still at school.

Much was expected of West Lothian as things got back to normal, but the following two years gave the *Gazette* many opportunities to comment on 'inept batting displays'. West Lothian travelled to the north of England in 1948 and had a creditable draw against Northumberland.

In the April of 1951 the decision was taken to play Sunday cricket at Boghall, and, perhaps of equal importance, the possibility of installing a bar at the ground was explored. It was a season of many ups and downs. No Counties Championship games had been won, but overall as many games had been won as lost. The next year continued in similar vein and with some noteworthy performances. Against West of Scotland, Jimmy Lidster's 99 included 13 sixes, thought at that time to be a ground record.

Fred Benham became captain in 1953. Willie Ellis had some very good games and his selection for Scotland was well deserved. Against Clackmannan a young Malcolm Ford made 34, including two sixes, and the first Counties Championship win in two years was recorded over Forfarshire. The *Gazette* reported, 'a spectator's hat went in the air to herald this long overdue win.' Against Forfarshire the next year, Jim Shanks and Tommy Watson put together a ground record stand of 184 in only 142 minutes. West Lothian visited the Borders for the first time, beginning an annual tour that continued for 20 years. In 1957, West Lothian won two, drew two and lost four in the Counties Championship. In 1960 Ford scored 941 runs, and it was no surprise when he earned his first cap. George Strachan led the bowlers with 67 wickets to his credit.

Malcolm Ford took over the captaincy from Jim Shanks in 1963. In that year things got decidedly better for West Lothian, with many ghosts laid to rest. The team finished second in the Counties Championship, having recorded five wins, three draws and three defeats. Donald Ford, younger brother of Malcolm, was now coming to the fore and finished the 1964 season with 821 runs in the book.

1965 was the year that everything came right for West Lothian. George Strachan was awarded caps against Ireland and MCC. After an early hiccup, there was a steady run of wins for West Lothian, with a range of outstanding performances as they won the Counties Championship for the first time, a feat well worthy of the civic reception they were given by the town council. Their outstanding form did not continue however, and the next year they slipped to third in the table. Malcolm Ford took his caps total to 17, when he was joined against Denmark by George Strachan and Andrew Reburn. In 1967 the club finished one up the table in second place. 1971 was not a bad season for the club, and good form was maintained in 1972, the Masterton Trophy being won for the first time. It is good to be able to say the Masterton Trophy was retained at Boghall in 1973 with a win over Grange. 1974 was a year of mixed fortunes, with eight wins, two draws and twelve defeats. The next year saw an improvement as the county moved to third place in the Counties Championship. In 1976 they started well, before fading away. West Lothian County won the Lowlands group of the Beneagles Quaich tournament introduced in 1977, but went out in the second round of the Masterton Trophy. The 16 year old Stephen Wilkinson scored 344 runs and took 19 wickets. Donald Ford took over the captaincy from George Strachan in 1978. Comment must be made on Kenny Scott, who at the age of 13 made his debut against Clackmanan in the Counties Championship with an innings of 26 not out. Also playing for the side that day was a 15 year old Gordon Hollins. West Lothian finished strongly that year, moving to third place in the Counties Championship. Looking back over 50 years in Scottish cricket there was cause for satisfaction. There was one Counties Championship, with many finishes as second or third. The Rothman final had been reached twice and the Masterton Trophy had been carried to Boghall on two occasions, while six players had been capped for Scotland.

1980 was a good year for the club, with the winning of the Gleneagles Quaich and the reaching of the Scottish final of the National Knock Out Tournament. The end of 1981 saw a notable honour come to the club as the late and much respected Cecil Kerr accepted the appointment of President of the Scottish Cricket Union, a position he filled with distinction. The next year saw early departures from the Quaich and Knock Out tournaments, but it is 1984 that demands our full attention. The Executive Committee Report for 1984 opens with these words:

> There is really only one way to describe 1984 – the best ever for the club. The winning of the Scottish Counties Championship for the first time since 1965 together with the retention of the Masterton trophy made it a season which will always be remembered.

In this remarkable year, Kenny Scott was awarded a cap against the MCC (he had earlier scored 203 for Scotland B against Durham University), David Fleming was selected for the Scotland B side and the bar achieved its largest ever net profit.

As so often happens in sporting clubs, as in life, a high was followed by a low and for a number of years the club had little playing success. Many prominent players left the district and there was a fall in the number of new members joining. The social side of club life held its own, progress was made with sponsorship, and in 1988 the district council installed a synthetic wicket. But the club faced considerable expenditure on clubhouse improvements over a number of years. New sight screens were installed, gang mowers were purchased for outfield work, and with the improvements to the clubhouse and changing rooms completed there was a feeling of satisfaction and optimism. Indeed the next year was to bring better rewards. Two district matches, two one day internationals and the SCU trophy final were all held at a very tidy looking Boghall. Perhaps more importantly, the club won the Caley 80/- Scottish Counties Championship and the Scottish Counties Knock Out Cup sponsored by the same company. This return to form continued in 1996 with the first eleven finishing as runners-up in the first year of the Scottish Cricket League and reaching the final of the Masterton trophy. The Sunday eleven also won the Forth Union Cricket League for the first time. True to form the Masterton finals were again reached in '97, as was a creditable position in the league.

Most noteworthy in '98 was the number of representative matches that were played at Boghall, a reflection on the tremendous work that had been done in raising the quality of the playing surface and the club's facilities. Such matches included Scotland against Yorkshire, Bangladesh, Australia A, and Ireland against England Amateurs. A good finishing position in the Scottish National Cricket League, Conference A meant the team would be competing in Division One of the league in 1999. And 99 could in turn be described as a fairly successful year. The club finished up around the middle of the National League, reached the semi-finals of the Scottish Cup, and true to form again got to the finals of the Masterton trophy.

West Lothian celebrated the millennium by winning the Masterton trophy and improving their position in the Scottish National League. And with a smile the whisky drinkers acknowledged the award of 'The Famous Grouse Team of the Month for May'.

Amateur clubs are at the mercy of players leaving the area for employment reasons and over the next two to three years the club was to be particularly hard hit. Declining fortunes saw West Lothian relegated from the National League to play in East League Division One in 2004. Yet looking back over 75 years at Boghall it is more appropriate to feel pride than despondency. The Counties Championship has been won three times and the Masterton trophy four times, with many appearances as runners-up. The coaching of youngsters, which has been so assiduously pursued over the years, brings promise of better times to come. And let us not forget the long list of players capped for Scotland from their home turf at Boghall:

Sandy Paris, Andrew Johnston, Fred Benham, Willie Ellis, George Strachan, Malcolm Ford, Kenny Scott, David Fleming, Omar Henry, David Orr, Steve Crawley, Ian Beven, Alec Davies, Gavin Hamilton and Sanjay Patel.

Linlithgow Ramblers and Hillwalkers

The early morning rucksack wielding groups that gather at the Cross at weekends, and their more genteel but equally animated brethren who parade at a later hour at Longcroft on Wednesdays, have one thing in common. They are devoted to the countryside in all its aspects and the hills in particular. The walk leader of the day will allocate cars and confirm the route to where they shall meet for walking. It is said, a trifle unkindly, that the Wednesday walkers always start from a public convenience and finish at a tea shop. The weekend walkers have slightly higher priorities.

It is almost 25 years since a walking group was set up and Linlithgow Civic Trust played an important part in its inception. In the early 1980s, concern was being expressed about countryside access locally. People were remembering that where Rights of Way were not being used they were likely to be lost for future generations. In the countryside it seemed that signs bearing the word 'Private', presumably meant to inhibit walkers, were on the increase. The first requirement of the Civic Trust was for some factual information, the second was to encourage people to make use of the tracks and paths where the community had traditional rights to walk. To this end a committee of the Trust invited well known walker John Davidson, who was serving on the committee at that time, to ascertain the

Ramblers Checking the Day's Route

position locally and present his recommendations. This was done, certain concerns were noted for ongoing attention and it was decided to start a series of walks concentrating on those footpaths where it was deemed appropriate the right to walk should be asserted. This indeed was a major step forward and the first walk was held in the autumn of 1982. The support was there. Nearly forty walkers turned out to make their way to the Union Canal aqueduct from Linlithgow Bridge and return to the town via the footpath. A programme of Civic Trust walks was now instituted through the winter months, the time when walkers had less need to worry about damaging crops and upsetting stock in the fields.

The Ramblers Association is the national organisation which co-ordinates and seeks to look after the affairs of walkers and its Linlithgow members were of course aware of the Civic Trust initiative. A feeling grew at Scottish national level that the time was approaching when a branch of the Ramblers Association should be formed in the town. This branch would be expected to have the strength to build on the Civic Trust's initiative. Following a number of conversations John Davidson called a public meeting in the May of 1986, when the decision was taken that a branch would be formed. Linlithgow Ramblers and HillWalkers were now to be recognised as part of the local scene. It was a decision that led the way to success over the years. Today the group has a membership of around 250.

So, what happens in a walking group such as Linlithgow Ramblers? The quick answer is, a great deal. A year round programme has to be drawn up that will attract the membership and cater for a wide range of walking abilities. Obtaining such a programme of walks itself is a considerable task. It involves reading books and press articles, picking the brains of friends and other walkers about where they have walked, a certain amount of exploration, contacting local and public authorities and, most importantly, studying the various trails marked on Ordnance Survey maps. Then, the walks themselves have to be categorised. This is important so that people know what to expect. It is also important because, as members of the National Association, individuals may attend the walks of other groups throughout the country, and many join the Linlithgow Group for an outing because of the popularity of its walks. Walks are graded as follows:

C:	Short fairly level walk of up to 6 miles.
C+:	Harder than the above, gradients involved.
B:	Medium walk from 6 to 12 miles. Boots required + food and hot drink.
B+:	As for B but more strenuous. Hills or longer distances involved.
A:	Hills over 2,000 feet or distances over 12 miles. Additional equipment and clothing may be required.
Slow A:	Taken at a slower pace than an A walk.
A+:	Very strenuous. Could require use of ice axe and crampons at discretion of leader.

Generally, Saturday and Sunday walks are for the more energetic and ambitious. Wednesday caters for the more socially inclined.

Each walk has a nominated leader who has volunteered for the task. It is the responsibility of the leader to be fully aware of the ground his or her group will traverse. This normally means the leader will have already walked the ground, or else they will carry out a reconnaissance beforehand. On the day, the leader will obtain a weather forecast, take action to ensure the starting point is known to all car drivers, set the mileage payment contribution, ensure that maps, mobile phone and first aid materials are to hand and cast an eye over the boots and equipment that arrive with the walkers. On the walk, he or she will lead from the front or arrange for that position to be covered, nominate a back marker who will know who has disappeared into the woods, hold the group into a reasonably compact body, keep an eye on the physical condition of all the walkers and select the pace that will be comfortable to the group, related to the expected time of return. The decision as to rest stops and meal times is the leader's, as especially is the decision to abort for weather or other reasons. All leaders on official walks are covered by the Ramblers Association third party insurance. But a leader should remember too that the group is walking for enjoyment and have a degree of toleration for those who like to have a look at the daisies as they walk along. Animal life, map reading checks, questions about a myriad of things are important to many walkers. Details of forthcoming walks are contained in the RA magazine *Trail*, which is issued twice a year. There can be slips between cup and mouth and the leader will advise if, for example, the published mileage differs from his own estimate.

The Linlithgow group spread their walks over much of Scotland. The Trossachs, the Borders, the Pentlands and Perthshire all have their devotees, as do the parklands and shore walks of Fife and East Lothian. The local area, with its concentration of history and places of interest is never neglected, and reference should be made here to John Davidson's splendid book of local walks. Even by only looking at a week's activities in the *Trail* magazine it can be seen that Munro baggers, hill walkers and local history types are being accommodated. But to many, the highlights of the year are those weekends when perhaps forty or more of the group take to the hills for some intensive walking. A hostel or hotel may be taken over *en bloc*, which allows common meal times to be followed by social evenings featuring music, song and dance. The current April to October programme features a weekend at Grassmere in the Lake District, a visit to Glen Affric, the Islands of Islay and Jura, Invergarry and Loch Ossian, and weekends at Braemar and Fort William. Colym Bridge has been a past favourite haunt and many will remember an outstanding New Year when the group took over the whole of the Youth Hostel in Pitlochry. It was a New Year that had everything.

Not all members of Linlithgow Ramblers do all their walking within the group. Many walk on their own or with a few friends, only making occasional contact with the group, and this fits in with the spirit of rambling. 'In the last twelve months club members have stretched their legs on weekend outings around Fort William and on the Island of Mull with a trip to Strathpeffer in the offing. Mention should also be made of the members who have raised considerable amounts for charity by means of sponsored walks. This includes a trek into the hinterland of Peru to reach remains of the Inca civilisation. Noteworthy is the Club's involvement in the national initiative 'Walking for Health' where shorter and slower-paced walks are arranged for the less able.' When Linlithgow Ramblers and Hillwalkers were formed in 1986, the objective was that the group would cater for the needs and interests of all who take pleasure in recreational walking. That group of anorak figures at the Cross would maintain that these objectives have been, and are still being, more that met.

Linlithgow Golf Club

Linlithgow Golf Club is sited on high ground at the west end of the town. The Union Canal and its allied rough form its northern limits. The views from the course are impressive and varied. To the north and west are the Ochil Hills, backed on a good day by the tops of Ben Vorlich and Stuc A Chroin. The slope of Ben Ledi is to the west, and further on Ben Lomond stands strong. Industry plays its part in the Forth Valley, as the eye takes in Grangemouth. The original nine hole course was laid out by Robert Simpson, the golf professional at Carnoustie, the town that boasts of providing the United States with more golf professionals than any other in Scotland. Simpson's expertise warranted a payment of five guineas plus expenses. The first greenkeeper was Robert Hughes from West Lothian Golf Club. He was hardly overpaid at £1.50 a week. At 5,359 metres the course is not long by modern standards, but it is tricky. Its longest hole is the appropriately named Lang Whang at 453 metres. Its shortest the 17th, which – presumably because of the number of balls which finish up in the canal – carries the soubriquet of 'Wishing Well'.

The club traces its origins to 1913 when, following a called meeting, 104 gentlemen, 67 ladies and 13 young people decided it was time Linlithgow had a golf club of its own and gave promise to join. The newly formed club managed to obtain the lease of an amount of land south of the canal at Braehead Farm adjacent to Williamscraig estate. Work on converting the fields into a golf course must have started right away as we learn the course and clubhouse were officially opened on 18 July 1914. The first treasurer must have had an astute streak. A ball stamping machine was purchased and all balls found on the course were returned to their owners at a charge of three pence per ball.

Ena Bennie, who has played the course since the late 1930s, has memories of pre-war days. Most members arrived for their game by cycling along the canal, leaving their bikes unpadlocked on the banks. Women waiting for husbands completing their rounds would sit knitting and gossiping on the clubhouse veranda. Granny Graham, who lived in a cottage on the site now occupied by the sheds, collected green fees and sold teas. Her son, who gave name to the trophy played for every May, became club captain and five times won the club championship. War, of course, meant change, and cattle grazed on the fairways and greens. Hostilities over, work began to make the land again fit for golf. In 1955 an alcohol licence

The First Tee and Professional Shop

was obtained, access to the so-called cellar being through a trapdoor in the floor.

Problems arose in 1955 when the lease expired. A new lease could only be obtained on a year to year basis, and a few years later the ground was bought by a local farmer who indicated his intention to revert the course to farmland unless the club wished to purchase it. The club could not meet the price and appealed to the town council to make a compulsory purchase. This was refused on the grounds that golf was available locally at the West Lothian Golf Club which was, as the crow flies, as close to the town as the Linlithgow Club. The Linlithgow captain, obviously a man of humour, retorted that 'the members were not crows but golfers, even if perhaps their golf was nothing to crow about.'

Help though was at hand. To the rescue came Mrs Gena MacKinnon of Williamscraig, the owner of Drambuie Liqueur. She bought the ground south of the canal and, although not a golfer herself, leased it to the club on a 20 year basis at a nominal rent. Mrs MacKinnon became Honorary President of the club and traditionally struck the first ball of the season. The club she used on such occasions is now contained within a cabinet in the lounge of the clubhouse. The course was eventually extended to 16 holes, being brought up to full size when Mrs MacKinnon again came to the rescue, giving the club additional ground to the west while retaining the right to graze her donkeys on it. This explains the name given to one of the holes: 'Donkey Lea'. Mrs MacKinnon died in 1974 and, after the estate changed hands, the golf course ground was bought by the club in 1977 at the cost of £34,000, the bank debt being cleared the same year.

Today the flag, which bears the club emblem of the Black Bitch supported by a Saltire of golf clubs, flies over a popular and well used clubhouse. There are 450 male members, 100 ladies and a strong contingent of 130 juniors. A five-day membership arrangement exists, as does social membership, and there is a waiting list of a 100 for full time membership. Ladies pay a reduced annual fee but have most voting rights and dedicated tee off times on Tuesdays and Thursdays.

Linlithgow Golf Club is a member of the Linlithgowshire Golf Association. The Association rotates its presidency round all the clubs in the county in turn. It is very keen on the promotion of junior events. The Linlithgow junior section has had outstanding success in recent years in county competitions.

The club is a member of the Scottish Golf Course Wild Life Group, which has the objective of overseeing golf course management in such a way that wildlife is protected and countryside beauty is maintained. To this end over 700 trees have been planted, and wildlife has been enhanced.

The club operates a full range of in-house competitions and welcomes many golfers from far afield to such Open competitions as Handicap and Scratch, Mixed Foursomes, Ladies Greensomes and events for Seniors. A golf professional has been in attendance for more than twenty years and there are practice facilities for all aspects of the game. A course manager and a number of well equipped green-keepers are employed, as is a bar manager. Support staff are brought in as required. The social aspects have never been ignored and the clubhouse has been extended over the years to meet the needs and aspirations of members. Two golf buggies are available for hire.

Linlithgow Bowling Club

Linlithgow Bowling Club goes back a long way in time. In 1865, a number of local figures decided the game should have a recognised home in the town. What bowling had taken place before that time is not known but the first green was established in the Boghall area, not all that far from where the Bellsburn Club plays today. Wall photographs record the scene in 1890. Twenty five years after its inception the club was to win the Roseberry Club, the trophy presented by Lord Roseberry and competed for by all the Linlithgowshire bowling clubs. It was not to be won again by the club until 1983.

At the turn of the 20th century the club moved to its present situation in Philip Avenue behind the West Port hotel. There, with the clubhouse stretching one side of the green and a stone and brick wall surrounding the other three sides there is an impression of compactness. The early buildings seem to have been fairly humble. The clubhouse was tiny, so small in fact that bowls had to be kept for many years in a caravan parked alongside. At one time the greenkeeper, one Jock Morrison, grew vegetables on the ground on which the club lounge now stands. Cars would be parked at the side of the green, their headlights allowing a game to be finished if the light was fading. In the 1950s membership was at the 100 mark, today it is 150. Ladies are admitted on an equal basis with men.

A look at the Honours Boards will show the club has achieved much. After the Roseberry trophy returned to the club in 1983 it again graced the trophy cabinet in 1989, 92 and 94. 1989 was a bumper year for the club, winning both the Scottish Fours and the Scottish Triples Championships. The Triple was won again in 1997. The club has been well represented at international level for both juniors and seniors. Malcolm Graham, Elizabeth Ann Wallace and Nicola Stein have brought international honours to the club, with Malcolm Graham becoming Scottish Junior Champion in 1981. The development of young players always seems to have been taken seriously within the club, no fewer than nine juniors going on to win the Senior championship in due course. Two members, Colin Stein and Allan Old, have established quite a record, both having won the club championship on five occasions. The club won the Kelso Cup in 1995. Wins in various county competitions are too numerous to mention. But worthy of a mention is the fact that no fewer than eighteen names appear on the club's Role of Honour for the 1914–18 War.

Surprisingly, a bar did not become part of the clubhouse scene until the mid 60s when the need for additional income made such an addition necessary. Until that time members made use of the West Port Hotel and readers who remember the charisma that emanated from landlord Iain McKay may understand why.

In the 70s, another Linlithgow character by the name of Sandy Dalrymple became president of the club and the drive was on to extend and expand the club's social activities. In 1974 the Dalrymple lounge was formally opened, the occasion being marked by a visit from the South African Touring Team. Welsh visitors were later welcomed, as was the Aberdon club from the north east of Scotland. In 1986, the team selected to represent Scotland in the forthcoming Commonwealth games, which included Linlithgow member Malcolm Graham, played against the club on its home ground.

The social life in the club is wide ranging. There is a monthly dance, talks are given on a range of subjects and coffee mornings are held. The Marches are acknowledged by a special lunch.

Linlithgow Sports Club

Linlithgow Sports Club, which occupies a wooded and sheltered location on the walk between Boghall and the town's shopping centre, offers facilities for pursuers of bowling, squash and tennis. Housed in a modern building with dressing rooms and a bar lounge it was formally opened in the July of 1982, having been built by a trust which comprised the Sports Club and West Lothian District Council. It is run by a board of management whose members are submitted by each section. The three sections, bowling, squash and tennis are autonomous, each having their own AGMs and committees. The fees are set by the Sports Club and members can join as many sections as they wish, but must pay for each at the going rate.

Named after the water that flows by the green, the bowling section is called Bellsburn Bowling Club. The club plays competitively against other clubs, has its own competitions, and gives much encouragement to young players.

The tennis scene

Although there have been facilities for tennis in the town in the past, it was not until the Linlithgow Tennis Club was established as part of the Sports Club in 1981 that one really got the feeling that tennis was about to become part of Linlithgow's sporting scene. Well sheltered by hedging and trees, Linlithgow Tennis Club occupies an attractive site in the Baron's Hill area of town. More than that, it is an active and thriving club with a successful record in the competition field.

Available for playing at present are four all-weather courts with a porous acrylic playing surface. Floodlighting is in place, allowing extended hours of playing. Indeed tennis is now regarded as a year round sport, and many families and others enjoy the game throughout the winter months. The club shares social facilities with the bowling and squash sections of the Sports Club.

Coaching is taken very seriously and the club's mini-tennis is accredited by the Lawn Tennis Association. There are typically 80 to 100 juniors and 'minis' in the programme at any time, and between 20 and 30 in the adult coaching programme, which caters for beginners, improvers and club players. There is a club coach in place to run these various programmes and offer personal coaching.

On the playing side the club has achieved much competition success. The men's top team is now to play in Division One of the Scottish National League and the club is planning for an extended run at this level. The senior and junior teams play in the Central Districts leagues. The men's first team in recent years has either been league winner or has finished in the runner-up position, while the six boys' teams consistently win or come close in their competitions. While not so successful as their male counterparts, the ladies' and girls' teams regularly occupy commendable positions in their leagues. On an individual basis, the club has also done well. The current top male player competes in the International Tennis Federation tour events, with a world ranking of around 800. Adult and junior members have also been selected at the British and Scottish representative level.

CHAPTER 10

Some Noteworthy Figures of the Town

Sir Charles Wyville Thomson

Sir Charles Wyville Thomson, the zoologist, was born at Bonsyde House, Linlithgow in the March of 1830. He studied at Edinburgh University and, after holding appointments in Aberdeen, Cork and Belfast, returned to Edinburgh as professor of natural history at the university in 1870. Bonsyde House has experienced a number of changes over the years and is currently serving as a hotel.

Wyville Thomson undertook various scientific dredging expeditions in the HMS *Lightning and Porcupine* in 1868–69. He is remembered today as the leader of the famous *Challenger* expedition of 1872–76. It was so named after the three masted, auxiliary steam Royal Navy corvette of 2,306 tons which set sail from Portsmouth to carry Thomson and his team of scientists over 68,000 nautical miles around the world, carrying out research at 362 stations.

The voyage was sponsored by the British government and organised jointly by the Royal Society and Edinburgh University, which was developing a reputation in Oceanography. The objectives of the expedition were extensive. They involved charting the depths and movements of much of the world's seas, identifying bottom, surface and intermediate temperatures, studying and collecting sea life at different depths, and prospecting by dredging for minerals on the sea bed.

Thomson was knighted in 1876 and presided over the geographical section of the British Association in Dublin in 1878. He died in Edinburgh in 1882. His writings included *The Depths of the Sea* and *The Voyage of the Challenger* in two volumes.

David Waldie

There must be many in Linlithgow who know where Waldie Avenue is but are unaware of the significance of the name. And there are many more who believe that the introduction of chloroform as an anaesthetic was solely the work of Sir James Simpson. Let us try to reveal the truth here.

David Waldie was a medical practitioner based in Linlithgow. He operated from the property now well known as The Four Marys – a plaque on the wall outside the hostelry acknowledges his former presence there. In the 1800s it was common for doctors also to be druggists and Waldie was particularly interested in drug research. He was looking for a safer agent to use as an anaesthetic than ether and, while undertaking research for the Liverpool Apothecaries Company, carried out work on refining the production process of chloroform to obtain a purer form. Everything seemed to happen in 1847. Waldie met Simpson, who was also actively looking for an improved anaesthetic, and recorded in a pamphlet:

> when in Scotland in October last Dr Simpson introduced the subject of an alternative to ether to me, enquiring if I knew anything likely to answer. Chloral ether was mentioned during the conversation and being well acquainted with its composition and with the availability and medicinal properties of chloroform I recommended him to try it, promising to prepare some after my return to Liverpool and send it to him.

A fire in Waldie's laboratory prevented him sending the promised sample. Simpson obtained some from another source and, after trials on himself and friends, used the new anaesthetic agent successfully in November of that year. While delighted with Simpson's success, Waldie felt his recommendation to experiment with chloroform had not been properly acknowledged:

> I did not feel inclined to go begging for more credit than he would be prepared to give spontaneously. Willingly do I acknowledge that the discovery was Dr Simpson's and the honour is due to him. But he might have given an honest acknowledgement of my part.

Waldie later moved to Calcutta, where he set up a manufacturing chemist's business. Back home, a silver Waldie Memorial Cup was purchased to commemorate the centenary of his birth. It is used annually as a Loving Cup at the Marches. Waldie's brother George became recognised as a writer and historian. A picture of the old chemist's shop in the High Street is included in Bruce Jamieson's book *Linlithgow in Old Postcards*.

Tom McGowran OBE

One did not have to be in the company of Tom McGowran for long before realising that there was something special about him. He possessed the assurance of those who know they are on top of their job; he carried the knowledge that allowed him to be listened to, irrespective of sphere, with respect; he shone with a vitality and exuberance for life; and in a very simple way his genuine interest in people encouraged them to respond to him with affection. He was a 'one-off'.

The son of an oil engineer, Tom was raised in Mexico, where his formal education was in the hands of his mother and his training for life was overseen by saddle weary cowhands. At the age of 12 he returned to Scotland and attended school in Edinburgh. The end of schooldays saw him join the *Scotsman*, moving later to the *Falkirk Herald*. His commitment to the newspaper industry started early and would continue all his life.

He volunteered for the army at the outbreak of war, was posted to the Far East and was present at the fall of Singapore. The fates would not be good to him. He was sent to work on the Death Railway in Burma and was involved in the construction of the bridge over the River Kwai. Now we come to a remarkable thing about Tom McGowran. At the end of hostilities, having suffered a most hellish time as a prisoner of war, he made up his mind that he could not allow hate of his captors to fill his life from thereon. His experiences would always be with him, frequently torture him, but he would not be overridden by hate. In later years when he met Japanese visitors he would volunteer directions and assistance, although he never indicated the roots of his ability to speak Japanese.

Returning to the *Falkirk Herald*, McGowran immersed himself in the newspaper industry. He read, as his wife Iris puts it, 'acres of newspapers every day', irrespective of language. He rose to become Managing Director of the *Herald* and then became involved in the growth of the Johnston Press as it set out on the takeover trail to become the substantial enterprise it is today. He scoured the world, especially the United States, seeking out the newest advances in technology and helping implement them in his organisation. His OBE was awarded for his services to the printing industry.

Tom McGowran never forgot he was a journalist. With an insatiable appetite for action he followed troops into action in Aden and Sarawak, hung out of an open-cockpit plane without a seatbelt to take photographs, and still found time to write books and lead campaigns, lecture and feature at conferences, and edit papers and magazines.

To his adopted home town of Linlithgow, Tom McGowran made a gigantic contribution. To the general public, he was the secretary of the community council. But he was much more than that, and much of his work was of a 'behind the scenes' nature. He was the instigator of Annet House, a prod that produced the theatre in the Academy, the opening up of the palace and Peel for banquets, son et lumière and jousting tournaments. Finally, mention must be made of his tireless work as secretary of the Scottish Far East Prisoners of War Association. Largely because of his agitations an award of £10,000 was finally made to survivors and widows.

Arthur (Pop) Brown MBE

Some characters take a long time to depart the scene. Although he died in June 1971, this former editor of the *Gazette* still works his way into conversations today. From all accounts he was a remarkable man, readily recognised by the cigarette, with its handsome portion of ash, which continually dangled from his lower lip. He seemed to possess but one car in his life, a 1925 Alvis that became as well known as he was. Incidentally, he was the father-in-law of Tom McGowran.

Born in Cumberland, his formative years were spent on his father's farm on the Buccleuch estates in Dumfriesshire. 1914 saw him in uniform, and from the blood and mire of Flanders he wrote articles about the war for his local paper, the Dumfries *Courier and Herald*. In 1916 he was badly wounded in the jaw, lock-jaw set in, and his life expectancy was not considered all that good. He returned to Dumfries and accepted the job of reporter which the *Courier and Herald* offered to him. There he continued until the Second World War came along. Then, because of staff problems and shortage of paper for printing, the *Courier and Herald* went out of business. Pop Brown was well known to Fred Johnston Senior of the Johnston Press, and he invited him to come to Linlithgow and become editor of the Linlithgow *Journal and Gazette*. A quick visit to the town convinced Pop it would be a good move.

Pop Brown was a great news gatherer. He did not wait for information to reach the office – he went into the streets and round the pubs digging out his stories. But his adventures were not yet finished. Towards the latter stages of the 1939–45 war he was given permission to visit the front line in Europe for a short period to collect material for his paper. With a newspaperman's nose he discovered the 'Crossing of the Rhine' was shortly to take place. When the time came for his return to this country he could not be found, he had disappeared. He was of course found eventually; on an amphibious vehicle crossing the Rhine. That was the good news. The bad news was he had picked up another wound, having received an enemy bullet in the head. Fortunately he survived and recovered.

Pop Brown never really retired from the *Gazette*. He retired as editor but continued to write 'the Pencillings' for a number of years. An enthusiast for the Marches, he instigated the family float, a lorry he and his family decorated early every Marches morning. He was involved for many years in the work of the Soldiers, Sailors and Airmens Family Association, and was awarded the MBE for services to the newspaper industry. His daughter Iris (wife of Tom McGowran OBE) also received an MBE for her work on Post Office National and Local Advisory Committees.

James Glen

Linlithgow can boast its full share of families that have made their mark in trade or public service, and many of these led lives that have captured the imagination. Such a family were the Glens, whose roots in the town stretched back to before the Reformation. Various Glens were provosts of the town from 1624 onwards and we see them associated with the lands of Longcroft. Alexander Glen, the father of James, made one serious mistake when he was provost. An enthusiastic Jacobite, he too readily espoused the arrival of the Chevalier in 1715 and found himself in retiral.

James Glen was born in Linlithgow and educated in the town and at Leyden. In due course he took over possession of Bonnytoun, and later the lands of Longcroft and Magdalens, which had belonged to his father. Public service became very much a part of his life. In addition to two spells as provost he was Watchman of the Salt Duty at Bo'ness and Inspector for Scotland of Seizures of Prohibited and Uncustomed Goods. In 1738 he was appointed Governor of South Carolina.

Glen may have thought dealing with Linlithgow's town councillors had equipped him with adequate skills in negotiation, but these skills and more were now to be required of him. France and Britain were struggling for supremacy and this meant that the support of the various native American tribes was essential for success. The tribes realised their position of strength and were not slow to play one side against the other. It was a time of great intrigue and subterfuge and Glen covered the colony, dealing with the various tribes of the Cherokees, Miamis, Ottawas and Senecas, all the while encouraging them to resist the lures offered to them by the French. His efforts were finally successful. In addition to Indian affairs, it was said Glen 'advanced the principles of constitutional government', drawing the line more sharply between its legislative, executive and judicial branches.

In 1743 Glen was appointed, in his absence from Scotland, Keeper and Curator of the Palace of Linlithgow and the Castle of Blackness. However, he did not leave South Carolina until 1761 and so missed out on the burning of the palace and the office of Keeper, which had become a sinecure. He lived for a spell in Cross House in Linlithgow and is credited with laying out terraced gardens on the west side of the Kirkgate. James Glen died in London in 1777, his body being brought north for burial in his home town of Linlithgow.

Stephen Mitchell

After the Union of the Parliaments, when Scotland was at last allowed to trade with English colonies, a new sight on the streets was that of pack-horses loaded with tobacco making their way to Blackness, from where the crop, which had been landed on the Clyde from such American colonies as Virginia and South Carolina, was to be exported to Holland. (Amsterdam was developing as a major tobacco centre.) In due course figures from the tobacco trade would take up residence in Linlithgow, the Mitchells, who later used a Black Bitch trade mark on their manufactured products, being the most famous.

Once again we come across a family involvement in the town – many of those who led the tobacco company, until it became part of the Imperial Tobacco Company, bore the Christian name of Stephen. The business line started in 1723, the year that, as well as commencing in the tobacco trade, one Stephen Mitchell was admitted a burgess and guild-brother. Other Stephen Mitchells would become burgesses in 1766, 1789 and 1817. The company is remarkable in that its trading lapsed at one time for over a hundred years but, on resurrection, was still able to put a Stephen Mitchell at the helm.

Much attention focuses on the Mitchell who founded the magnificent Mitchell Library in Glasgow, widely regarded as one of Europe's greatest. Born in Linlithgow in 1789 and educated at the Grammar school, he gained an apprenticeship with a merchant company where he bound himself 'not to frequent taverns or keep company with idle or disorderly persons, play at cards or other expensive games.' He took over the business on the death of his father. Manufacture continued in Linlithgow until 1825 when, Blackness losing its right to trade in tobacco by the Excise Authority, the company was forced to move to Glasgow where tobacco could be freely imported.

Sandy Dalrymple

Every town has its kentspeckle figures, men and women who seem to express the town's identity and character. One such figure in Linlithgow was Sandy Dalrymple. A Black Bitch, Sandy's main scholastic achievement seems to have been the award of a watch for perfect attendance. He served his time as a butcher, saw war service in the RAF and, returning to 'civvy street', bought a small newsagent's business. This, his first shop, was in due course demolished, and he later took over two other shops in the High Street.

With a strong open face, he was known to everyone. His humour was positive. One Marches Day, coming across a stationery Clydesdale horse, he mounted it and rode bareback in the procession, fully kitted out in Dyers' morning dress. His passion was bowling and he was the driving force behind the extending of the Linlithgow Bowling Club, the lounge of which bears his name. But he was involved in much more in town life. He seemed automatically to be a member of this and that; curling, cricket, junior football. He spoke regularly at Burns Suppers where his humour was in demand. He versified, and kept a watching brief over the activities of the old town council.

1974 saw local government reorganisation take place in Scotland. An impassioned believer in his town, Sandy was the speaker at the Marches Day breakfast. He gave that day what some who have attended many breakfasts claim to be the finest of such speeches they have ever heard. But at the end of it, his humour took over:

THE DEMISE OF THE TOWN COUNCIL ON REGIONALISATION

Lord Wheatley as a Minister was given the call
To blow up the contents of our modern Town Hall;
All Black Bitches are we; to the Cross we did flock
To see the last rites of the auld Toon Clock.

The building went up with a jam and a bang,
While we stood looking, we drank and we sang,
You'll see by the *Gazette*'s last written minute
The Provost and Council were all sitting in it.

The sky all lit up with sparkle and flame
As aff tae the moon went Dean O' Guild Bain,
While sitting on high just playing a harp
Was the last that was seen of Treasurer Clark.

We roared and we laughed and all shouted gaily
As in the Cross House landed our junior Baillie,
While Wade, Glen and Merker had just one desire
To get off the church, where they hung on the spire.

Then McGinley and Marshall they'll tell you thersel'
Were lucky to land head first in the Well.
And o' Baillie Cook, next Provost he thocht
Was spread out in bits – all over the Loch.

But what o' the Provost – he's no to blame,
As he swung from the flagpole by ermine and chain,
Then a hush in the crowd, which showed no regret,
The town foreman has found the boots of James Flett.

While Mel Gray and Roxburgh at the end of the table
Were blon right oot through the eastern gable,
And when we enquired just where they had gone,
We found them next door, at the Feast of St John.

What have we got left just Hogg and wee Ford
They landed weel doon for free rent and board;
For the job that they do little talent's required
To stoke up the flames of the big burning fire.

Then for an encore, with entertainments – Thom,
We strapped him astridelegs to a muckle big bomb
And if we should meet him, our hats we maun doff,
Saying – 'Here's to the councillor with his members blown off.'

So, thank you, Lord Wheatley, you've done very well,
You've blown all our Council right up into Hell,
Who'll look after us now and act as protectors?
Colonel Ponsonby, nae doot; and a' his objectors.

Margaret Laidlaw

Margaret Laidlaw, wife of James Hogg, 'the Ettrick Shepherd', came to live in the town after her husband's death and frequently gave readings of his works.

Sir John Moore

Not a drum was heard, not a funeral note
As his corpse to the ramparts we hurried,
Not a soldier discharged a farewell shot
O'er the grave of our hero we buried.

Sir John Moore, the hero who was killed in his moment of victory against the French at Corunna in January 1809 during the Peninsula War, served as Member of Parliament for Linlithgow in 1784–85.

CHAPTER 11

Linlithgow Twinning Association

THE TOWN TWINNING movement was born in Europe shortly after the end of the Second World War. Some twinning arrangements grew out of a local regiment's association with a particular place, some because of trade inducements, and others because they saw educational, social or other benefits accruing from contact with a village, town or city in another country. In formal circles the concept is described as 'getting to know and understand each other better'. Today, around 200 places in Scotland have entered into twinning arrangements.

Linlithgow can boast of having one of the most active and competently run twinning associations in Scotland. Its record of achievements in terms of exchanges and initiatives is second to none. Not that the early years of the Association were without difficulty; there were problems aplenty. But industry and enthusiasm carried the day and many thousands of all ages have gained much from their twinning experience.

Our story starts towards the end of 1983, when Mairi McFarlane, the then head of the Academy's modern language department received a copy of a letter from the Paul Eduard school in Guyancourt, an expanding town a few miles from Versailles in France. This letter was addressed to schools in the Edinburgh area and it enquired about possible student exchange. In the Academy the letter fell on fertile ground, so fertile indeed that in the June of 1984 pupils from the Paul Eduard school could be seen walking around Linlithgow in the company of Academy pupils and their parents. A few weeks later Academy boys and girls were being hosted by Guyancourt families. These educational exchanges continue to this day.

While the Academy and the Paul Eduard school were contemplating the logistics of student exchange, Linlithgow's community council was giving thought to a wider arrangement that would meet the needs of the town's people in both specific and general areas. The council envisaged a full twinning arrangement with a town somewhere in France. A net was cast but early approaches were not productive, something that turned out to be a blessing in disguise as an unexpected letter arrived from the Mayor of Guyancourt. Impressed by the success of the school exchanges that had taken place, the Mayor proposed a twinning arrangement should take place between Guyancourt and Linlithgow.

One would have thought that this proposal would have been greeted with great joy but this seems not to have been the case. Although letters were exchanged over the next few months, the vote on 28 May 1985 was only passed by six to five in favour of formalising twinning arrangements. Not a very good omen, one would think.

School exchanges continued to be popular and in 1986 three visitors from Guyancourt became the first of many to take part in the Riding of the Marches. But the road ahead was still not clear. The community council, having agreed to a twinning arrangement, discovered it had not access to sufficient funds to finance the venture. With a fine disregard for the community council's problem the Rugby Club organised its own trip to Guyancourt to allow its attendance at an international there and shortly afterwards the important and rather bold decision was taken to form the Linlithgow Twinning Association, which was to be independent from the community council and to stand on its own feet. The first committee included some well known and active citizens:

Chairman – Ian Donaldson
Secretary – Margo Watson
Treasurer – Clare Pollock
John Ferguson, Fraser Findlay, Jimmy McGinley and John Watson

From 4 to 6 December 1987, 50 people from Linlithgow took part in the first official visit to Guyancourt. Working closely and harmoniously with the Twinning Association's French equivalent, *Le Comite de Jumelage*, formal twinning ceremonies took place in Guyancourt in 1988 and in Linlithgow a year later, the latter event happily coinciding with a visit by Her Majesty the Queen. The Guyancourt Mayor, adorned with a tricolour sash, was strategically placed in the palace policies so as to receive a special acknowledging smile from the Queen. Early twinning arrangements saw biennial exchanges instituted between the Paul Eduard school and Linlithgow Academy, and between Guyancourt and Linlithgow Rugby Clubs, the latter trips not unsurprisingly timed to coincide with the France-Scotland rugby internationals. From now on, the Association *and Le Comite de Jumelage* would organise biennial visits to Linlithgow and Guyancourt every Easter time. These visits would develop personalities of their own.

A quick comment about Guyancourt: driving through the town today one is first struck by its modernity. New housing prevails, sometimes married to classical architecture. It is spacious and good use is made of trees. As with all new towns, it takes time to comfortably find one's bearings. Not that the town is all new. Its history stretches back over a thousand years and until some 30 years ago it was

GUYANCOURT VENNEL

This plaque was unveiled by
M. Roland Nadaus
Maire de Guyancourt
Linlithgow's twin town in France
on 15th June 1998

VENELLE DE GUYANCOURT

Town Twinning. From left to right: Ian Donaldson, Chairman, Linlithgow Twinning Association; Provost Joe Thomas, West Lothian Council; M. Roland Nadaus, Maire de Guyancourt; M. François Deligné, Maire-Adjoint de Guyancourt.

Photograph: Ian Donaldson

a village in the countryside with a population of only 1,500. Then things began to happen. In the 1960s it was decided a new town should be built to the south west of Paris. This new town, to be called St Quentin-en-Yvelines, was to be, and now is, made up of seven separate 'communes', one of them being Guyancourt. This promoted expansion in Guyancourt, industry moved in, new housing was built and the population of Guyancourt is projected to rise ultimately to 38,000. Yet there certainly remains in parts of Guyancourt a rather pastoral ambience and care has been taken to retain the original village features. Guyancourt's location has much to commend it. It is within a ten minute drive of upmarket Versailles, with its famous château and gardens. Versailles is a notable spot for those with a need for retail therapy. It also provides the rail link into Paris and without changing trains one can travel direct to such attractions as the Eiffel Tower (near which a boat trip on the Seine is readily available), the Musée d'Orsay, Boulevard St Michel and Notre Dame, as well as the important rail station of Austerlitz. Hosts invariably seek out their visitors' prime interests and make every effort to meet their fancies.

A word about travel to Guyancourt. When the twinning was in its infancy, journeys – including coach and ferry crossings – demanded a robust constitution. The opening of the Channel Tunnel was a major improvement and it is now possible to leave Waverley station, Edinburgh at a respectable hour in the morning and be in Paris by five o'clock that afternoon. Some travellers fly of course, but coming quickly to the fore in the popularity stakes is the Rosyth-Zeebruge ferry, with a connecting coach to Guyancourt. Not because this is the quickest route, but because of the interaction it allows between those travelling. Music, song and a quiet drink at sea are tempting bedfellows.

Some years over 300 people make the journey between the twin towns. Some have a genuine interest in meeting people from another country, a desire to expand their horizons or to improve their French, or just like to travel and socialise. For others, the priority is to pit their talents or prowess against new challengers in a novel environment. Let us look at these two categories separately.

For the socially minded, a twinning visit offers the opportunity to see the lives people live in other countries, the food they eat, their outlook on life, and – and this is sometimes accompanied by surprise, if not shock – how they regard those domiciled on this side of the Channel. It is essentially a happy experience, meeting a French family round the table and being entertained at dinner dances and concerts. Both Linlithgow and Guyancourt have shown that their people have amazing talents. Housewives turn into cancan dancers and agile youngsters tread the boards, while choirs and musicians range from folk to the classical. The acquisition of knowledge is painless and stretches from wine and cheese tasting and learning to play boules, to folding napkins for a party and visiting places of historical and cultural interest.

Visitors to Linlithgow from Guyancourt have explored Edinburgh and Stirling Castles and Falkland and Linlithgow Palaces, danced in Hopetoun House, experienced a fiddlers' rally, a ghost walk and a civic reception, and gone to such interesting places as St Andrews, Stirling and New Lanark. In France we have sampled the known and unknown delights of Paris and towns such as Rouen, Vaux le Vicomte, Chartes and Auvers – forever associated with Van Gogh and the Impressionists. And with a little pride, we have introduced the French to the world of Burns Suppers, silently thanking our forefathers for translating the Bard's works in advance of our requirements.

Some, of course, have eschewed the formal arrangements and sought their own entertainments. It is said that Scottish coinage from Linlithgow pockets has made its way into the Tote at the Prix de l'Arc de Triomphe – the famous Paris horse race – on more than one occasion.

Among those who journey to Guyancourt in pursuit of their sport or hobby, pride of place must go to Linlithgow Rugby Club. The club's connection with Guyancourt Rugby Club goes back to February 1987, when some 50 members and friends travelled to watch the France-Scotland international and play their first game on French soil. The Rugby Club's mini fraternity have also enjoyed Guyancourt hospitality.

Tennis and golf have also featured in the exchanges. The Judo Club has had regular contact since 1993 and Linlithgow Rose Football Club and Baillielands Football Club have also carried the flag across the Channel. Artists from both towns have had their works displayed in exhibitions. When on top of all this one remembers the continuing contact of an educational nature – ranging from school exchanges and work experience to primary school letter writing – as well as the many informal visits paid due to developed friendships, one begins to realise the extent and value of the Twinning arrangement. Truly, the Auld Alliance is alive.

But our twinning story is not yet finished. Indeed one wonders where it might end.

About two years after the formal agreement between Guyancourt and Linlithgow was signed, Guyancourt entered into a twinning arrangement with the Bavarian town of Pignitz. Delegates from Linlithgow were invited to attend the ceremony. A friendship link then developed over the years with representatives from Linlithgow attending the bi-annual visits between the two continental towns. In the course of events, delegates from Pignitz were welcomed to Linlithgow when it was the turn of the French town to pay its bi-annual visit. But there was more to come. Nearly two years ago the German town entered into a twinning agreement with Slany in the Czech Republic. Again, delegates from Linlithgow found themselves being warmly welcomed at the meetings between the new twin towns. And this is where Scotland's Bard enters the scene.

People from Linlithgow have twice crossed the Channel to perform at a Burns Supper in Guyancourt. On the first occasion it should be noted, speaking solely in French. Between these two events a Burns Supper was held for Guyancourt folk in Linlithgow, when a Pignitz visitor brought the house down with a rendering of 'Willie Wastle'. Now came an inspired suggestion. There should be a Burns Supper in Pignitz during the formal Guyancourt visitation which would also be attended by delegates from Linlithgow and Slany. It came to pass in the January of 2006 when those who had the good fortune to be present are not likely to forget the experience. Tam O' Shanter in three languages!!! That's one for the Guinness Book of Records. The Pignitz response has been to offer an Oktoberfest in Linlithgow in November 2007.

What parents can do it seems the children can match. In the week leading up to the 2006 visitation to Guyancourt pupils from Linlithgow, Guyancourt and Pignitz schools showed their musical talents when they presented a marvellous concert. This is to be repeated in Linlithgow during Easter 2007 when pupils from Slany will also be present. Pupils from Linlithgow Primary School who have already paid two visits to Guyancourt intend to make it three consecutive years in 2007. It seems the knot between the peoples of Europe is ever getting tighter.

CHAPTER 12

Linlithgow Civic Trust

UP TO SOME 30 odd years ago, Linlithgow's High Street was part of the roadway system which linked Edinburgh with Central Scotland. In the 1960s, tempers were short as drivers of heavy vehicles and cars attempted to progress down a street clogged with traffic. Apart from some shopkeepers, who feared a loss of trade, everyone was relieved by the news that a motorway was to be built between Stirling and Edinburgh, bypassing Linlithgow. It seemed like the answer to a prayer.

But as details of the proposed line of motorway percolated through, there were murmurs of discontent. It lay immediately to the north of the loch as it passed Linlithgow and many thought the noise of the traffic would not be diminished but possibly enhanced by the open space of the loch, and would reach an unacceptable level in the town. And it was not only the noise that would detract from Linlithgow's desirability as a place to stay – countryside views would be impaired, the walk round the loch ruined, and bird life affected. There was no shortage of arguments against the proposed motorway line.

The answer of many of those expressing their antagonism was to move the line of the motorway further north, into the hollow before Bonnytoun Hill. A grass roots movement got under way, with the feeling that the Scottish Civic Trust might be a useful ally in a fight against the Scottish Office (which had agreed the line). A meeting took place and was chaired by Mrs Julia Wade, herself a member of the Linlithgow town council. It cannot be said that all the members of the council were pleased that such a meeting had been called – some felt their authority was being usurped. They were in a difficult position as the motorway was outwith the boundaries of the town. But the meeting decided that action was necessary and before long a local Civic Trust came into being and was making its feelings known to all and sundry.

In addition to the line of the motorway, the question of access came under review, and we still suffer in Linlithgow today because the importance of easy access to the motorway for westbound vehicles from the east end of the town was not realised. In any case, the fight to have the motorway moved north was not successful and it came into being on 18 December 1972. But the newly formed Civic Trust action group did have a voice in putting forward suggestions to limit the sight of the motorway from the town and to baffle its noise by means of intelligent landscaping and the planting of trees and bushes.

Whilst the members of the action group had not succeeded in their primary objective of changing the route of the motorway, they did feel they were doing something useful. They also felt the building of the motorway could not be treated as an isolated event and that other instances would arise where an organised group, whose members were concerned and informed about the history and amity of the town, could, and should, make constructive comment about proposed developments. On these grounds the decision was taken to form a permanent Civic Trust.

The new Civic Trust, under the able Chairmanship of the late Lt Col C B (Chum) Ponsonby, was fully aware of the need to resolve the conflict between, on the one hand, the careful preservation of the town's historical and traditional characteristics, and on the other hand, the considerable demand for modern facilities, which are all too easily achieved by needless redevelopment. They were not alone in this. Throughout the land similar groups were questioning the attitude that old buildings were bad, with no place or use in modern times, and should therefore automatically be demolished to make way for new. Already this had happened quite extensively in Linlithgow, as elsewhere. People were beginning to realise that through the efforts and persuasions of such groups, and with a little time and effort, old buildings could be rescued and made fit for new uses; that this need not always cost more, and that most people would actually prefer the results.

The fledgling Civic Trust was soon given the opportunity to make formal comment on many planning and development matters. Buildings of 'Special Architectural or Historical Interest' were being 'listed' so that the authorities had extra powers to preserve or enhance their character and appearance. Wider areas were being designated 'Conservation Areas' where collectively, if not individually in every case, their buildings and other features made them of historical or architectural interest. The Civic Trust made suggestions and recommendations for such listings in Linlithgow and gave comment when it was consulted on the Local Authority's proposals for the town. Comments on planning proposals within Conservation Areas or on Listed Buildings are given in conjunction with the West Lothian History and Amenity Society, which also comments on proposals elsewhere in the county.

The Civic Trust has been active in a wider role in relation to planning matters. It has given evidence and presented local opinion at public enquiries. It has responded to major development proposals outwith Conservation Areas and the creation of successive Local Plans with considered analysis and constructive comment. The Trust is concerned with encouraging sensitive development and opposing the inappropriate.

The Trust has been involved in a wide range of other activities. It has held talks on many matters within its sphere of activity and arranged visits to places of interest. It has hosted exhibitions and made awards for good design. It has organised tree and bulb planting on the town's approaches and, more recently, actively promoted the Burgh Beautiful campaign to improve the town's appearance through planting in such places as the railway station and the Low Port. One welcomes the new town entrance, and tourist signs, which incorporate the Burgh seals at the Trust's suggestion. The Trust has produced and published a whole series of booklets on subjects ranging from local walks, through advice on trees for small gardens, to local place names. In 1974, the Trust published *A Brief Architectural and Historical Guide* to the town, a publication it has since revised and reprinted. Its more recent publication *Linlithgow Old and New* deserves acclaim for its wonderful collection of photographs.

The public face of Linlithgow Civic Trust is currently very prominent. There is a fuller appreciation of the Burgh Beautiful campaign and what it offers as the planters, tubs and flowerbeds add colour to the town. The decision to enter the Beautiful Scotland in Bloom competition was a bold one and it was recognised success would not come easily. But such was the effort put into the entry that success did come, the town achieving third place in the medium size town class behind Cupar and the section winners Forres. One applauds too the efforts of local schoolchildren and the St Michael's Parish Church Embroiderers to brighten the interior of the station building with their flower tiles and banners.

Looking to Linlithgow's future, one recognises the need for a more dynamic momentum than what currently exists and a clearer concept of where we are going. The Civic Trust's ideas for the future as set out in their 'Vision For Linlithgow' document highlight the failure of the present policy of development restraint, and, recognising the inevitable expansion of the town point to what has to be done if Linlithgow is to retain its character and attractiveness and meet the people's needs in the years ahead. Delivered in summary to every house in the town, this is one letter-box arrival that warrants our serious attention.

We in Linlithgow are fortunate it is home to such an active Civic Trust, committed to preserving and enhancing the unique and distinctive character of our Royal Burgh.

CHAPTER 13

Linlithgow Heritage Trust

Annet House – home of 'The Linlithgow Story'

SOME 150 YARDS down the High Street to the west of the Cross a somewhat olde world sign advising the home of 'The Linlithgow Story' projects from a square grey-brown building. This is Annet House, the town's museum. The house has a history going back to 1787. Originally it served as a private house, before being taken over by the West Lothian county council in the 1930s, acting as the base of several different departments in turn. At the end of the 1939–45 war, in a gesture which in many ways typifies the town, a group know as the 'Welcome Home Committee' was formed to acknowledge the contribution and sacrifice of those who had served. A dinner was held in the Victoria Halls, at which gifts (cigarette cases to the men,

The Herb Garden at the Rear of Annet House

compacts to the ladies) were presented. But the committee, with considerable vision, wanted to have some kind of community focus established as a permanent memorial to those who had served, and to this end purchased Annet House from the council. But it was to be some years before the house became a museum.

Since at least the late 1800s a small museum had existed in the Burgh Halls, pride of place going to the town's historic weights and measures. Once one of Scotland's most important towns, Linlithgow had been charged with the responsibility of keeping the standard measure for weighing oats, barley and other grains. This measure was known as the firlot. Every other burgh in the land had to ensure that its measure for grains was checked against the Linlithgow standard firlot, and each was branded with the Linlithgow branding iron. The little museum also held liquid measures, as well as the important bushel, which when filled with oats would indicate to a miller the amount of oatmeal that could be obtained. There was also a sword reckoned to have connections with the battle between the Douglases and the Lennox faction, the site of which is now marked by a cairn on the road leading to the leisure centre. Other bequeaths arrived over the years but when local government reorganisation came along in 1974, and burghs technically ceased to exist, the contents of the little museum were placed in the charge of the Royal Museum of Scotland in Edinburgh.

Linlithgow is a town where grass roots movements flourish and in the 1980s there was a thrust for the establishment of a museum that would portray the extent of the town's history. A Museum Trust was formed and entered into negotiations with the now entrenched West Lothian district council, but it took some years before the council agreed to make Annet House available as a museum and the funding was granted for the required internal structural work to be carried out. At the back of the house there is a garden running down to the old town wall and it was seen that this offered possibilities as a visitor attraction. In 1991, the Trust was reconstituted as Linlithgow Heritage Trust and took over the development and running of the museum.

Today, thanks to the honest toil of a number of committed volunteers, Linlithgow can show its museum with pride. On the ground floor there are displays telling of the historical background to the town, its royal connections and its history as a Royal Burgh. These are supported by an audio-visual display. Efforts are made to bring important aspects of Linlithgow life to the attention of the people in the town and short term displays and exhibitions are often set up on the ground floor. Moving up the stairs, one becomes involved in the trades of the town over the centuries. These range from the old occupations of shoemaking and tanning to those of the more recent past. Crafts, trades and industries are dealt with elsewhere in this book, but mention should be made of the video presentation in the museum on the process of linen manufacture.

A striking exhibit on the second floor concerns the Scotch Brigade; the magnificently restored colours of the Brigade have at last found an appropriate home.

Scottish regiments and mercenaries have a long history of involvement in Continental affairs and a Scotch Brigade formed in 1572 served the governments of the Netherlands for 200 years, as well as seeing service in the United Kingdom. The government army which met Claverhouse at Killiecrankie contained several regiments from the Scotch Brigade. The association with the Dutch ended in 1782 and some officers of the Brigade, on their return to Scotland, offered to raise a new Scotch Brigade to serve exclusively with the British Army. This new Brigade served with great distinction in India and subsequently saw service under Wellington in Spain and Portugal. The town's association with the Brigade was strong.

Major-General Ilay Ferrier of Belsyde, a grandson of Sir William Hamilton of Westport and Belsyde was responsible for raising the new Brigade. It is said he persuaded the entire Linlithgowshire militia to join up. Ilay Ferrier's nephew then commanded the Brigade in India. William Jamieson, Town Drummer of Linlithgow until his death in 1850, served with the Brigade in Spain and Portugal. The drum he used for his official duties, which can be seen in Annet House, is decorated with the battle honours of the Brigade (the 94th Foot as it was later known).

When passing through the door at the back of the house one sees, dramatically situated at the foot of the garden, a statue of Mary Queen of Scots. The late Tom McGowran, who did so much to guide the fledging idea of a museum to fruition, was a great admirer of Mary Queen of Scots and was devoted to the idea that she should be appropriately recognised in the town of her birth. To his memory the stone is dedicated.

The Heritage Trust participates in Scotland's Garden Scheme, and gained many friends and plaudits after appearing in the popular BBC programme, *Beechgrove Garden.*

The garden itself extends over three terraces behind the house and has been planted with the varieties of vegetables, herbs and fruit

The Statue of Mary Queen of Scots in the Garden of Annet House

(neatly phrased as 'plants for cooks, apothecaries and brewers' on a board in the garden) that might have been grown at the time the house was built. It is well worth a visit, if only to pause by the stocks and jougs.

A number of activities take place in Annet House. There is the Annet Lecture, which takes place every February and is given by a person of national standing. Dramatic presentations based on incidents in Scottish history, usually with a connection to the town, are frequently given, and occasional pamphlets published. The Heritage Trust is active in the tourist field generally and is registered by Visit Scotland as a visitor attraction carrying the noteworthy three star classification.

Objects of interest continue to arrive at Annet House and a recent acquisition is a Medieval Skillet which was found at Parkley Place Forum. Ever keen to increase people's involvement with the Trust an 'Adopt an Object' campaign was recently launched. This has been a most successful initiative both financially and in obtaining offers of expertise.

CHAPTER 14

Lithca Lore

ENTHUSIASM FOR LINLITHGOW is not confined to its traditions or its historical past, nor is it parochial in texture. But as a plant needs sustenance, so enthusiasm needs injections to allow it to evolve gracefully in a changing world and not live completely in the past. This means merging the old with the new; it also means exposing the contribution that the townspeople make to life in this Ancient and Royal Burgh.

It was in 1985 that two fairly young Black Bitches realised an aspect of town life was being passed by; some of the immediate and recent past was not being recorded and was therefore liable to drift from memory. In addition, little was being done to promote the writings and poetry of local folk, which could enhance both life and interest in the town. Thus *Lithca Lore* was born, the brainchild of Forbes Walker and Murdoch Kennedy. It would be a publication that merged the old and the new, a vehicle for those with a story to tell in prose or verse, an end product for those prepared to research a local item they deemed worthy of their time and attention.

To date six booklets have been published and it is worthwhile looking at some of the gems of the past and present they contain.

The fourth booklet told the story of the Linlithgow Bridge footballer, George Allan, a star centre forward who was Liverpool Football Club's first Scottish internationalist. As a result of this article appearing, Linlithgow Bridge community council was inspired to suggest staging in his honour an annual seven-a-side football tournament for local primary schools. With the support of Linlithgow Rose Football Club this event is held at Prestonfield every May and involves boys and girls from primary schools in Linlithgow, Linlithgow Bridge, Bridgend, Winchburgh and Whitecross. Thus in a modern context the past is kept alive.

Many ex-service men and women will read with interest, and perhaps other feelings, the splendid and well documented article in the sixth booklet about the local Territorial unit, the 14th (West Lothian) Light Anti-Aircraft Regiment of the Royal Artillery. Locally known as 'The Terries', the 39th Battery of the Regiment was based in a drill hall next to the cemetery, across the road from the Rose Club. This article, which deals with the Battery's involvement in North African campaigns, and later activities at Salerno and Cassino in Italy, is worthy of very wide circulation.

After the surge of battle
The crash and roar of guns
Welcome! A thousand welcomes!
West Lothian's valiant sons!
Our hearts were always with you
They followed you everywhere
And that God safe home would bring you
Was the burden of many a prayer.

Since 1985, *Lithca Lore* has made a notable contribution to the Marches, and its entries illustrating local themes have become a popular feature of the Marches procession. An early decision was taken to highlight the *Lore* team's passion for Linlithgow's heritage by hiring a horse and cart and portraying a scene from the past. This was intended to mirror the Marches of former times, when participating Trades and Craft fraternities had distinctive styles of dress and decoration. A sense of nostalgia has been present in many of the *Lithca Lore* entries over the past 20 years – these have included 'Auld Worthies', 'Ghosts of the High Street', 'Lithca 1943', and '1745 – Ye Jacobites By Name'. In more recent years the group has used a vintage lorry supplied by local contractor Tom McPhie and humorous themes have included the hilarious 'Eastenders at the Marches'.

Lithca Lore has done much to heighten awareness of the Marches traditions and encourage people to become involved. Some of the group's former Deacons are now playing a significant role in the Deacons Court, helping to organise the biggest occasion of the year in the town.

Importantly, the *Lithca Lore* group has revived many old poems and songs written by locals such as Robert Fleming, Ebeneezer Oliphant, Peter Middlemass, Willie Fortune, George Charleston and Andrew Hunter. Without *Lithca Lore* it is doubtful if most of these works would ever be read today. In 2004, at the instigation of *Lithca Lore*, Robert Fleming's most famous song, 'Here's Tae the Marches' was recorded by the popular local folk group, the Black Bitch Band. As well as reviving old material, *Lithca Lore* has produced a modern slant on the old traditions with new poems, songs and anecdotes. Among the most notable of these is Forbes Walker's 'The Five a Cloke, Six a Cloke, Seven a Cloke Roke'. The old and the new!

Finally, mention should be made of *Lithca Lore*'s involvement in reminiscence work with the senior citizens of the town. It works closely too with the Linlithgow Folk Festival Association in organising evenings of entertainment in local sheltered housing complexes.

The Quest for the missing Black Bitch

The aforementioned Forbes Walker has a story to tell. It is a special story, one that emphasises the commitment of Black Bitches to their town, not to mention the cussed and determined streak that can be found in some of Linlithgow's inhabitants. Forbes now lives in Carnoustie, on the wind swept shore of Angus. There the *Gazette* is still regular reading and one morning, on reading the 'Down Memory Lane' column he came across the following:

> ...in reply to the query about the Cross Well, what is said to be part of the old well stands in the gardens at Pitmedden, Aberdeenshire. There is a central pillar bearing sculptures of St Michael's head, the Black Bitch, and the inscription 'My fruit is Fidelity to God and the King.' The pillars were presented by the Ministry of Works to the National Trust, and erected at Pitmedden in 1955.

Forbes reminds us that the first Cross Well was built in 1628 and required some repairs after suffering damage from Cromwell's troops. Pieces of that old well have been found in the palace. The current Cross Well was built in 1807 by a one-handed Edinburgh mason called Robert Gray, who worked with a mallet strapped to the stump of his other arm. Excited at the prospect of seeing a relic of Linlithgow's past, Forbes made for Pitmedden. Sadly, he was in for a disappointment. Adorning some pieces of stone was a plaque:

> Given by the Ministry of Works. Seven fragments of the Cross Fountain of Linlithgow. Erected at the Restoration of Charles the Second, and set up here in the year 1956.

But where was the expected Black Bitch, its supporting column and other stonework? Forbes made contact with both the National Trust and Historic Scotland seeking information as to how the stones had arrived at Pitmedden in the first place and wondering if the Trust would return the stones to their right-ful resting place in Linlithgow. Little progress was made. Historic Scotland could give no information on the transfer of the stones to the National Trust, while the Trust maintained all was in order. A further request to the Trust for information elicited the reply that two sections of the central pillar had been removed for tech-nical reasons. The reply went on to say that 'sections of the stonework had been stolen from the property and never located.' It continued:

> ...should they still exist, the NTS would like to point out that the stones were gifted to Pitmedden garden by the Ministry of Public Buildings and Works, under the

supervision of a former Inspector of Ancient Monuments in Scotland in the 1950s and as such, are the Trust's property which it is committed to keeping for the benefit of the nation, and the Trust has no intention to sell or gift the stones back to their original site.

Forbes was not to take this as a final answer and set out to publicise his cause. The *Gazette* gave its attention to the search and Linlithgow Heritage Trust promised a welcome to the stones should they be returned to the town. Our story has a happy ending. Some two years later, Forbes again made contact with the National Trust. This time he was advised that while some of the fountain had been vandalised, the so-called missing pieces of stone were safe in an outhouse and could be inspected. And at a later meeting attended by Forbes, Alan Young, the late Tom McGowran, and a National Trust representative, it was agreed that the stones would be returned to Linlithgow. Today they are in Annet House for all to see.

CHAPTER 15

Charities and Support

Linlithgow Link

TO MANY, ranging from the housebound and lonely, to under-pressure mothers and those needing help to get to hospital, Linlithgow Link is the most important organisation in the town. Its story is one of how local people have responded to an identified need.

It was in the late 1970s that District Nurses became aware of an increasing number of elderly housebound patients who were suffering from a lack of contact with other people. Loneliness is not a pleasant state and these District Nurses brought their concern to their Nursing Officer, the late Isa Morrison. She in turn, realising the community implications of finding people to visit the housebound, raised the issue with the Reverend Ian Paterson of St Michael's Parish Church in the town. They were to be a formidable team. The need for a voluntary group was quickly established. In 1979, Linlithgow Link, the first organisation of its kind in West Lothian, came into being. A Steering Committee was formed, with representatives from District Nursing, police and the community under the chairmanship of Ian Paterson. Isa Morrison was appointed liaison officer.

The fledging organisation needed much. It needed volunteers, a co-ordinator, an office arrangement and some funds. Five public-spirited citizens offered themselves as 'Linkers'; Joy Macintyre as secretary, complete with typewriter, offered to work from her house. And by selling some of her garden produce, Isa Morrison opened a bank account with seven shillings and six pence. The Link was in business. Within five years the register of volunteers grew from five to 85.

The early work of the Link focussed on visiting the housebound and helping with related chores such as shopping. Inevitably this caring service was extended to include younger people. Linlithgow is a growing town drawing its increasing population from all over the UK. Many young couples arrive in the town without any local ties. Young mothers with a new baby to look after are often unable to call on relatives to babysit while they have a break from family responsibilities. This was a fertile field for Link to develop.

Shortly afterwards, one of the most important activities undertaken by Link, the Car Service Scheme, was developed. People in the town requiring out-patient hospital attendance have a problem. There is a limited public transport service between Linlithgow and St John's Hospital in Livingston and various medical centres in Edinburgh and it can barely be called satisfactory, especially when considering the age and physical condition of many of those requiring to be transported. An appeal was made for volunteer drivers using their own cars to drive people to the appropriate medical centre, for which a mileage allowance was to be paid. Volunteers wait while the patient receives their treatment, before returning them to their home. This valuable service is well used. In 2005, some 630 journeys were made.

Linlithgow Link is involved in many social activities that do not make the headlines. Those confined to bed in such places as St Michael's Hospital welcome Link visitors. 'Pat-a-Dog' visits, the Linker providing the dog, have given much pleasure to many. Social evenings are run in the hospital during the winter months, to which patients can invite their friends and relatives for a refreshment and a programme of entertainment. In 1990, a Link Abbeyfield Support Group was formed to provide a regular social afternoon for the Abbeyfield residents. Senior Citizens from the community, who mostly live alone and are unable to get out much are also invited. These people are taken to Abbeyfield by Link drivers, to enjoy entertainment, a cup of tea and home baking, and above all, companionship. An annual Burns Lunch has become quite an institution, volunteer drivers again transporting those in need. The Wednesday Club is the name now given to what was formerly the Post-Natal Exercise group crèche, with Linkers taking over the role of baby minders. The Link is active too in the town's sheltered housing complexes. In Brae Court, calls of 'house' may be heard at bingo sessions, and a weekly gentle exercise class operates. At the West Port home a Linker helps with the lunch club and visits are made to residents. The Link continues to look for new ways to brighten up the lives of the housebound. One recent innovation worthy of development is the organisation of outings to places of interest or beauty, for which vehicles capable of accommodating people in wheelchairs are hired.

Inevitably where volunteers work so wholeheartedly, humour can be found. There is a story worth telling about the St Michael's Christmas Party of some years ago. Some volunteers decided to present their version of the popular TV programme of the time, *Come Dancing*, which was hosted by Angela Rippon. One of the barmen (actually the Link auditor), having a rush of blood to the head, dressed himself in fish net tights, a stunning gold dress, wig and make-up, to lead the dance team on to the floor. The dancers were lady Linkers, and their partners were life size dummy figures they had made themselves at home. The show was a great success. At that time the Convenor of West Lothian district council was the much liked James McGinley, known to all affectionately as 'Jimmy the Chain'.

One of the non-human dancers was obviously meant to represent the Convenor. Never slow to miss an opportunity for humour, the Convenor sought permission to borrow the figure, which finished the night dancing at a council Christmas party.

As in so many charity organisations the funding of the Link's services is an on-going tale of sweat and worry. Initially many overheads were carried by the volunteers. Mary Clark, the first co-ordinator operated the administration from her home, as did Joy Macintyre, who took over the appointment after three years. But by 1985 it was obvious that the organisation had reached the stage where a properly equipped office was necessary to cope with the work load. The battle for financial support had now reached a critical level. It is interesting to see where some of the funding came from:

1986   an award was received from the Andrew Carnegie Trust.

1987   the Liaison Officer won the Royal College of Nursing Community Nursing Award. Isa Morrison used this money to purchase a Computer for Link.

1988   there was a financial crisis. A public collection brought in £800, which allowed Link to survive for a year. On the credit side, Lothian Health Board offered Link a room in the administration building of St Michael's Hospital.

1989   the Voluntary Co-ordinator Joy Macintyre was presented with the Whitbread Community Care Award by Her Royal Highness the Duchess of Kent, allowing Linkers' cars to be equipped with child seats. Since 1986, attempts had been made to receive Local Authority funding. Indeed on one occasion Isa Morrison and Joy Macintyre attended Lothian Council Chambers in Edinburgh to beg for £300 to meet the cost of Link's telephone bills but were not successful. But their perseverance paid off and in 1989 funding was granted for running costs and in 1992 there was further funding to meet the costs of part time co-ordination staff.

Help also came from many local organisations and individuals in the community.

In 1997, Barbara Bruce took over from Joy Macintyre. Although Link now receives funding from the West Lothian Social Work Voluntary Organisation Budget, the organisation itself continues to raise funds to meet its needs, and one notes especially the success of the sponsored walk which, started in 2001, is now an annual event.

On 3 June 2005, Linlithgow Link was named West Lothian Voluntary Organisation of the Year. Looking back over the more than 25 years of tremendous effort for the community, no one can deny it was a well deserved honour.

Laetare International Youth Centre

It was, one would have thought, the least auspicious time possible to establish a hostel to cater for the needs of young people from different countries. Yet, in the dark years of the Second World War, that was exactly the vision of a remarkable man. The man was Father Michael McGovern, the priest in charge of St Michael's Catholic Church in Linlithgow. The hostel he was to establish and which would achieve a world-wide reputation stands within the church's policies overlooking Linlithgow Loch.

Father McGovern gave his hostel the name 'Laetare', which means 'Be Joyful' in Latin. Accustomed to working with young people, Father McGovern had a deep faith and what might be called a simple philosophy. He was convinced a person's social and recreational needs are so much part of their human make-up that Christianity cannot ignore them. He had already had success in developing activities that would satisfy the recreational needs of the young; there was a special emphasis on discussion and debate in addition to physical fulfilment. Right from the beginning he sought to make Laetare a place where the whole body and spirit could achieve renewal. As he was later to say, 'To conquer the world for Christ we must first set out to get all we can of man – both body and soul.' His later experiences – meeting refugees from Germany and young girls sent to Laetare after release from forced labour camps – served to reinforce his belief in the necessity for his work. In a newspaper interview, Father McGovern told how the idea of a Catholic youth centre of scale had come to him when he was working in close contact with some of the worst slums in Scotland. Its urgency had been hammered home in the course of a talk he had had with a German priest-professor, a fugitive from the Nazis. The priest had spoken of conditions in the Hitler youth camps, which he described as 'the breeding grounds for irreligion'. Father McGovern was convinced too of the value of travel in a person's development, while recognising that such departures from the family hearth cause parents much concern. He saw Laetare as a place where young people from other countries could base themselves for a while, their parents recognising they were in a secure environment.

The hostel's beginning was indeed modest. In 1942 Laetare started life in a small two bedroomed cottage, six girls being welcomed through its doors. The demand for the limited accommodation was remarkable, no less than 500 bed nights being recorded in the small hostel's first season. Two years later another cottage, now known as Lochside Lodge, was acquired, which allowed boys to share in the hostel experience. But it was with the end of hostilities that the hostel began to fill its role as an international meeting place for young people. Now comes the story of an amazing coincidence: amongst the first visitors were two girls from the States. A few years later, Father McGovern travelled to New York and, while there, visited a youth club. To his surprise, there were the two American girls – scheduled to show a film of Lochside Lodge and encourage their friends to visit Laetare.

It was on his return from the States that Father McGovern was given the opportunity to submit his long term plans to the Diocesan Finance Committee. He had been asked by his Archbishop if he had seen anything worthwhile in the youth movement in the States and whether he now had any further development in mind. He quickly replied he had plenty of ideas but no money. He submitted his plans and the necessary loans were approved. By 1948, plans were accepted for a twin hostel for boys and girls on ground which had been occupied by Polish soldiers during the war. June 1949 saw the new Laetare open its doors. Records for that summer show a weekly intake of 120 boys and girls and some 500 men and women. In the seven years since the centre opened, over 16,000 bed nights had been recorded. Almost in parallel, a new St Margaret's Hall came into being. Again, it is an amazing story. This much larger hall – with a seating capacity of over 300 – occupies the site of an old hut adjacent to the hostel and was completed in 19 days utilising four fifths of the materials of the original hut.

The hostel was now to become a major focal point in Linlithgow life and the people of the town became accustomed to seeing groups of young people chattering away in different languages walking the streets. Interest in the work being undertaken was increasing and bus parties from other parishes were arriving to gauge for themselves the success of Father McGovern's approach to renewing body and soul. Prominent visitors included the then Secretary of State for Scotland, the Right Honourable Arthur Henderson. The facilities by 1949 were excellent, with football and hockey pitches, tennis courts, putting greens and a volley ball court augmenting the indoor facilities of dormitories, dining room and lounge. The *Journal and Gazette* found Laetare a source of news and regularly commented on the concerts and céilidhs and camp fire sessions that were taking place. Laetare had become the largest youth scheme in post-war Britain. In due course its work would be referred to by UNESCO.

The official opening of the modernised Laetare took place on 13 January 1951. After the from all accounts splendid dinner prepared in the hostel kitchens, Linlithgow's Provost, Crawford Lamb expressed the town's thanks to the centre and its staff for the help and accommodation given to the townspeople who had been made homeless by the recent fire in the High Street.

As a celebration, 17 August was declared an International Day and in its acknowledgement Consuls from France, Spain, Eire, Belgium and Holland were present, together with visitors from Germany, USA, North Africa and Indo-China. The young people from fourteen different countries staying in the hostel at the time celebrated with sports, folk singing and dancing. A week later, West Lothian council honoured Laetare with a civic reception in the Burgh Halls and presented a table for the reception area of the centre.

1955 was a boom year for Laetare as it welcomed its 100,000th visitor on a bed and breakfast basis. And still young people poured in from all over Europe, North America, Australia and Africa. Older groups of people were now common-place as the centre was being referred to as an 'informal university'. Laetare had always enjoyed a good press at home and now one could read articles about it in French and German papers. A March 1960 article in an Australian paper said:

> Thirty thousand young people have stayed there since its opening in 1949, and it would be difficult to find any country of the world or any town in Britain that is not represented in its Visitor's Book.

1967 saw Laetare celebrate its Silver Jubilee, at which many spoke about the con-tribution the Centre had made to Linlithgow life and how it had extended the town's name and fame throughout the world. But there was another Silver Jubilee to be acknowledged. Father Michael McGovern was presented with the Queen's Silver Jubilee Medal in 1977 in recognition of his services to youth. This medal he donated to Laetare, where it can be seen today by the entrance door. Father McGovern died on 4 July 1980. The good work at Laetare continued for another twenty-five years after his death. Then it became obvious the hostel building was nearing the end of its working life and a massive amount of money would be required for a replacement building and the continuation of Father McGovern's work. At this point in time it can only be said that a very special era has come to an end, an era which will remain strong in the memories of many.

Seeds of Hope

St Michael's Church, the parish church of Linlithgow, was consecrated by David de Bernham of St Andrews on 22 May 1242. Towards the end of 1991, there was much discussion as to how the 750th anniversary of this consecration might be celebrated. There was initially no great consensus as to what would be appropriate, but one man had an idea. The story of the fruit that grew from the idea is well worth relating.

The 'Iron Curtain' that had stretched across communist Europe had been torn down a year and a half earlier. There was a general awareness in this country of the deprivation that existed in Eastern Europe. A feeling existed locally that more contact, more direct help could be given to these countries now struggling to establish new economies on a grass roots basis. If this could be done it would be both a humanitarian gesture and a useful way of acknowledging St Michael's 750th anniversary. Into focus as a place where help could be given came an orphanage in Romania.

With support from a Christian charity called 'Caring for Life', a group of four took the road to the city of Arad in Western Romania. They were, from St Michael's Parish Church, Marshall Green and Tony McLean Foreman – the then associate minister – and from St John's Evangelical Church, Jim Cockburn and Peter Johnston. Their intention, which they carried out, was to give practical help in the refurbishing of the orphanage. The effect on the four who went was profound. Not so much because of the deprivation that was seen and the needs encountered but more because of the instant friendships that were formed with people who had struggled under the oppressive Ceaucescu regime for more than 20 years. Following their practical refurbishment work, the group arranged a youth exchange (followed later by school exchanges) between the two Linlithgow churches they represented and a church in Arad. This first exchange was followed by the sending of a convoy of two mini-buses and a 7.5 ton truck of medical goods and clothing donated and packed by people of the town. Such aid has continued over the past thirteen years.

Such travels produce anecdotes, not to say crises. Marshall Green tells the story of one party of 14 Romanians coming to Linlithgow on a convoy return leg. They had an uneventful journey across Hungary, Austria, Germany and France. Then, at eight o'clock one morning, a telephone call was received in Linlithgow advising their engine had 'blown up', they had no money for train tickets and didn't know what to do. Within the hour arrangements had been made for them to get on the connecting train to Peterborough, where they would pick up the London-Edinburgh train. When they arrived at Peterborough a British Rail employee met them on the platform with their tickets. But what of their minibus, and how were they going to get home? Radio Forth came to the rescue. Their predicament was broadcast and within an hour an Edinburgh garage volunteered to rebuild the engine for free if the minibus could be brought to them. Again, Radio Forth came to the rescue. The station contacted the AA, who agreed to bring it north without charge. Within four days the bus had been brought north, the engine rebuilt, and it was returned to the Romanians. The leader of the Romanians later said, 'I did not believe anything like this could ever happen anywhere in the world. It was a miracle.'

It was after handling large sums of money donated by people in the town and other parts of West Lothian that the now expanding group decided to form a Scottish registered group, initially called 'New Life'. This was later changed to 'Seeds of Hope Charitable Trust', and its activities considerably extended. From its first project helping with the refurbishment of an orphanage, the Trust moved on to giving support to a health clinic in Romania, and to a Romanian charity called Children for Christ. This has become a major activity. This charity provides a six day camp for around 400 underprivileged children every year in the village of Virfurile, and as well as financial assistance the town sends ten tons of aid and 700 'shoebox' Christmas presents every November. A Seeds of Hope farm has also been set up in Romania. This farm is concerned with offering work and accommodation to orphans and street children and also gives assistance to local peasant farmers, whose cultivations are restricted because of lack of machinery and capital.

Seeds of Hope have now extended their work to other countries. After Louis Muvuny had completed his studies in Scotland and returned to Rwanda, money was subscribed from the area, allowing him to set up a school catering specifically for the children of families decimated by the genocide of the 90s. Two school buildings have now been completed and the first nine children enrolled. Following the Tsunami disaster in 2004, the charity became involved in a rehabilitation project to provide low interest loans to fishermen in India. Forty fishermen and their families have been helped so far and it is interesting to note that a third of the money dispatched to date has been donated by Scottish fishermen.

'Seeds of Hope' has done a remarkable job in taking the name of Linlithgow to some unusual places in the world. Where opportunities arise the charity intends to continue to reach out and come alongside in faith to plant 'Seeds of Hope'.

CHAPTER 16

Beecraigs Country Park

Beecraigs at its Tranquil Best

BEECRAIGS COUNTRY PARK lies a very few miles to the south of Linlithgow as one drives towards the Bathgate Hills. Heavily timbered, it occupies around 1,000 acres and is a favourite walking and general outdoor pursuit place for Linlithgow people. Its recent history is one of constant development and improvement.

The history of places within and near the Park, especially Balvormie, Whitebaulks and Beecraigs, can be traced back to the fourteenth century. A charter of 1345 mentions the lands of Ballormy, of which one John de Malevil seems to have become the owner at that date. In 1607 the Patronage of the Altar of St Andrews was given with the Temple Lands of Balvormie and Whitebaulks to David McGill, ownership changing in 1690 to the Earl of Linlithgow. By 1850 we know that there were kilns, a limestone quarry, and a brick and tile works at Whitebaulks. During the First World War German Prisoners of War built Beecraigs reservoir on land now owned by the Duke of Hamilton. Then, in 1921, the old Linlithgow council bought Balvormie and Whitebaulks and the first plantings took place as shelter belts round the reservoir. The council of course did not have the intention of creating a Country Park at that time. The focus over that period was the importance of the reservoir as a supply of water and the South Eastern Water Authority and Lothian regional council would each in turn become involved in its management. In due course West Lothian county council took over responsibility for the reservoir and in 1967 the Countryside Scotland Act provided the enabling legislation for the setting up of Country Parks. In 1976, the county council appointed a country parks manager and in 1980 Beecraigs Country Park was registered with the Countryside Commission for Scotland and came officially into existence. The development of a recreational facility now became a major objective. Car parks and a basic system of tracks were built, planting was undertaken and the public was encouraged to visit the recreational facility on its doorstep rather than further away attractions.

Beecraigs, since the 1920s, has had its fishing devotees. Indeed it was a favourite haunt of Sir Harry Lauder. Initially clients competed for the hire of the two boats on what was essentially a brown trout loch. Then thought was given to the rearing of trout both for stocking the loch and for sale to the public. The farming of rainbow trout was instituted and this has been a highly successful venture. It is recorded that an almost unbelievable three tons of trout was sold in one day, in a scene reminiscent of the January sales. Eight boats now cater for the needs of fishermen. The catch record now stands at twelve fish weighing in at 118lbs. The largest trout taken out of the loch weighed over 28lbs.

For many, the greatest initiative undertaken at the Country Park was to begin deer farming. Today such farming is fairly commonplace but that was not the position 20 odd years ago when deer farming pioneers were scarce on the ground. There was a feeling that deer would be more of a visitor attraction than sheep. The bold decision was taken, and a number of deer calves obtained from the island of Rum. The initial herd flourished and today some 500 head of deer can be seen in the Park. The reputation of the herd too has flourished, and stock has been exported from Beecraigs all over the world for breeding purposes.

Hand in hand with these commercial enterprises was the establishment and development of what has come to be known as Environmental Education. Talks and field studies have long been associated with rangers' duties, the badger watches at night being particularly popular. But Beecraigs staff have sought to incorporate more active pursuits into their curriculum. Most walkers in the park will have come across the archery target range. Less obvious is the field archery arrangement, where archers using longbows and recurve bows must pit their skills against targets

The Deer Farm at Beecraigs

sprung suddenly into view. This is a worldwide competitive sport and the park has hosted two European championships and a World Championship. Courses in canoeing and kayaking are also available, while for those interested in orienteering, prepared maps and information sheets can be had. A recent venture has been to take learners off-site to practice skiing and snowboarding skills when required conditions are not present in the park. The play area for youngsters has long been popular, with much use being made of the Flying Fox and the Climbing Spider.

Beecraigs is heavily wooded, with a wide range of species of broad-leaves and conifers. Wind damage to the trees is often severe and damaged trees and thinnings make their way to the small sawmill, where fence posts and other small scale items are produced. Many species of tree may be seen in the park and it is good that the Scots pine is present. The mixture of trees is important to the park's squirrel population, with both reds and greys making homes there. The more aggressive greys are happiest in hardwood plantings, while our shy indigenous red likes to roam amongst the cone-bearing species. Wild roe deer are sometimes seen in the park, foxes very often, and the area carries a good badger population. An interesting experiment of a few years ago was the use of pigs to clear an area of ground for re-seeding, taking advantage of their natural rooting habits. Turning to plant life, mention should be made of the grassland at Balvormie, which is managed for the benefit of the greater butterfly orchid which grows there.

For the sake of visitors to the area a start was made in the 1980s on the building of a well-designed caravan site. This has proved to be a most popular venture. Today the site offers 56 pitches and has been highly commended in caravan publications. Direct labour was also responsible for the building of the Beecraigs Restaurant, which operates on a franchised basis. On the outskirts of the park, but on council land, one comes across an unexpected and most unusual building. It is worthwhile parking the car and paying the building a visit. This is the Scottish Korean War Memorial. The British Legion had for some time been searching for a suitable site for such a monument when a member thought the landscape at Beecraigs reminded him of Korea. Building soon followed.

CHAPTER 17

The Trades, Crafts and Industries of the Town

ON A PILLAR in St Michael's Church is suspended a beautifully made sampler, stitched by local embroiderers, which depicts the trades of the town. It gives a useful pointer to the crafts and trades that were being pursued in Linlithgow in the 1600s, when the population was around 2,500.

Eight incorporated crafts were in existence in the first half of the 1600s. These were:

The Bakers, who also made and sold ale.

The Cordiners or Shoemakers. Initially they also tanned the leather but in due course tanning developed into a sphere of its own.

The Coopers, who were not only involved in making barrels, but in a range of wooden vessels.

The Smiths or Hammermen, the metal workers of the town, who made swords and spears, and served the agricultural and commercial communities.

Tailors, who were said to have had an aura of superiority, making ornate dress for the well-to-do as well as clothes for the ordinary people.

Weavers, who worked mainly from home, specialising in coarse linen.

Fleshers – butchers who did their own killing – sold their meat at the market at the Cross.

Fullers or Cloth Walkers, who were concerned with the finishing of cloth. Their work was probably taken over by the dyers in the late 1600s.

Wrights, who were associated with cart manufacture and general joinery and repair work.

There were many other occupations which were not, at least at that time, accorded incorporated status; dyers, carriers, glovers and masons, candle-makers and carters for example. Such people were not allowed to stand for election to the town council until the end of the seventeenth century.

Each Guild elected a representative known as the deacon, and from these deacons one was selected to serve on the council as Dean of Guild, responsible for the maintenance of trading standards.

The minting of currency took place in the town, corn mills were prevalent and there was local brewing and distilling. But Daniel Defoe, the writer of *Robinson Crusoe* and a secret agent for the English government prior to the Act of the Union of the Parliaments, placed a different emphasis on occupations when he visited the town:

> At Lithgow there is a very great linen manufacture; and the water of the lough or lake here, is esteemed with the best in Scotland for Bleaching or Whitening of linen cloth: so that a great deal of linen, made in other parts of the country, is brought here either to be bleached or whitened.
>
> The whole green fronting the lough or lake, was covered with linen cloth, it being the bleaching season, and I believe a thousand women and children, and not less, tending and managing the bleaching business.

Unfortunately little in trade stays static for long and, as cotton came to the fore, so Linlithgow's linen yarn trade declined. But by way of compensation leather was becoming of increasing importance to the town. It is often claimed that the early tanning carried out in the town produced an inferior article until some of Cromwell's soldiers imparted the tricks of the trade to the locals. But the most accurate disclosure of the work being undertaken in Linlithgow arrived in the early 1790s with the publication of the government-inspired Statistical Account, which commented:

> Though Linlithgow has not that appearance, a good deal of business is being transacted in it. The people in general are sober and industrious, plying their occupations chiefly within doors, or on the side of the loch. The manufacture of leather is the most extensive and advantageous carried on here. There are employed in it, 17 tanners, 18 curriers and 13 tawers (converters of skins into white leather by use of mineral salts).

The Account recorded the importance of shoemaking, showing that a hundred shoemakers were turning out 24,000 pairs a year, many of them being exported to America. Two tambour factories were now in existence and up to 200 were being employed in calico-printing. Bleaching was said to be active, while snuff, although being milled at Muiravonside, was being traded from the town.

The Account commented on the excellent quality of porter, ale and beer being issued by the three breweries but was not so generous in its praise of the four distilleries. Five mills catered for townspeople's needs and it is good to know that even in these days the bread was considered remarkable for its fine colour and delicate taste. Eels from the loch were being transported as far away as London.

But beauty, they say, is in the eye of the beholder. Twenty years later a professional travel writer by the name of Wraxall would comment, 'The town seems dull and destitute of any manufacture or trade.' And he did the tourist trade little favour by writing:

A more villainous inn than MacKenzie's in Linlithgow I believe Scotland cannot produce. We were nearly starved in it, and indeed were starved out of it, for we quitted the place at two o'clock on Sunday to return to South Queensferry because we could get nothing to eat in Linlithgow.

In social terms, life was getting better. An Act of 1840 prevented, or rather reduced, the number of children being sent up chimneys as sweepers. Children under twelve were not allowed to be worked for more than nine hours a day. The Board of Supervision of the Poor in Scotland, when reporting that the physical condition of the children in Linlithgow poorhouse was unsatisfactory, recommended the introduction of 'more active and joyous games' and that the children should be taken out for exercise two or three times a week. Professor Smout, in his *History of the Scottish People*, quotes a sad statistic: 'No less than 25 per cent of the work force in West Lothian was under the age of thirteen.'

The next Statistical Account was compiled in 1843 and refers to the leather trade in its various branches as 'the staple of the town.' No fewer than 24 boot and shoe making concerns are listed, employing over 300 people. Those engaged in tanning appear to have been considered slightly superior in status. They earned 13 shillings a week compared with the shoemakers' 10 shillings and worked two hours a day less than the shoemakers' twelve.

As for the rest, the single distillery is described as 'extensive', and there are two glue factories and a brewery. Of particular interest to us because of its later importance to the town is the mention of an apparently highly productive paper mill now being in existence, as well as a large calico-printing establishment. Quarries are being worked at Kingscavil and East Binny, the latter remarkable for its bitumen, from which especially bright burning candles can be made.

In less formal terms, William Hutton, in his tale *Simon Moneypenny*, gives his industrial overview:

Though the manufacturing of leather and shoes are now the staple trades in the Burgh of Linlithgow, this was not always the case. Tanning had a very early origin, and, less or more, has been carried on with varying success for a very long period. Bleaching, skinning, heckling, and woolcombing have flourished alternately at one period or another, and weaving also was carried on to a pretty fair extent. But the sound of the shuttle is now nearly silent. The weaving trade is being represented by one solitary loom, and its humble occupant may be safely reckoned, the last weaver o' Lithca.

The Third Statistical Account, which was published in 1892, shows a significant change in the character of the town. No longer are leather and shoemaking to the fore, the Account claiming the local craftsmen were unwilling to change their practices and their produce. Gone too are the grain mills and the stone quarries. The ability of industrial concerns to grow in order to satisfy a market and then, irrespective of apparent strength, decline as conditions change has been amply illustrated in the town. Nobels, the manufacturers of explosives, set up a factory to cater for the needs of the shale industry in 1904. Twenty years later their Regent works were absorbed into ICI, which, on the decline of the shale industry, switched the factory's production to pharmaceuticals. Today the factory is no more, a supermarket, shops and some offices occupying the ground which at one time offered work to around 450 people. Sad too is the loss of the town's prominence as a paper-making centre. To others it is more significant that St Magdalene's distillery, with a history going back to 1800, should have endured the conversion into apartments, the present bonded warehouses not providing the same solace.

Anyone driving through West Lothian today will see a number of reddish coloured bings, the spoil heaps that proclaim the shale oil industry that once dominated the county. It is difficult to believe today the number of mines, works and refineries that were such a part of life here for a 100 years from the middle of the nineteenth century. This was the land of Paraffin Young, the man who founded the world's oil industry.

Linlithgow was slightly out of the source area, but the Linlithgow Oil Company was formed in 1884 to mine the estates of Champfleurie (the field of the flowers) and Ochiltree. According to David Kerr's *Shale Oil Scotland* it was anticipated there would be a 40 years supply of shale at 1,000 tons per day.

There was nothing half-hearted about the company's approach. An oil works, retorts, a refinery, a candlehouse and a railway were built around Champfleurie and Bridgend. By 1885, 500 tons of shale a day were being produced. But within two years there was a series of setbacks. Production problems, market prices, a strike and a fire caused the company to fold. A takeover resulted and the company continued to trade for a number of years. Until the shale industry disappeared locally in 1962, the town provided its share of labour, workers' buses regularly leaving in the morning for open cast or underground destinations.

As Racal Defence Systems and Sun Microsystems settled in the town, one wondered if Linlithgow was to be incorporated into Silicon Valley. The former company has departed the scene, however, its site being earmarked for a specialist school. One is tempted to say that construction is the main industry in the town today as, following the building of umpteen estates over the past 40 odd years, new houses are continually appearing, many in places one had never thought of as offering building possibilities. And of course, house extension is a thriving market.

Linlithgow offers much to the tourist in pursuit of history and recreation and is a key area for expansion. Much more, one feels, could be done to the palace. Providing the Great Hall with roofing would open up many possibilities for entertainment. Field and watersports are still capable of expansion. Specialist shops are making a contribution, while individual initiatives such as ghost walks, guide-book walks, country dancing, and the Riding of the Marches provide reasons for visiting the town. The success of the Falkirk Wheel has meant increasing activity on the Union Canal. But hand in hand with these initiatives must go good town housekeeping and development for inhabitant and visitor alike. And that, as they say, is another story. Can we meet the challenge?

Bibliography

Anon, *A West Lothian Miscellany*, West Lothian History & Amenity Society, 1983

Anon, *Linlithgow Marches*, Court of the Deacons of the Royal & Ancient Burgh, 1981

Anon, *Linlithgow Palace*, Historic Scotland, 1996

Adam Babtie, 'Linlithgow Loch as a Bird Sanctuary', 1996

A.M. Bisset, *The Poets and Poetry of Linlithgowshire*, John Menzies & Co., 1896

George Bisset, *Official Guide to West Lothian*, 1997

John Davidson, *Walks Around Linlithgow*, Linlithgow Civic Trust, 1999

Adam Dawson, 'Rambling Collections of Past Times', *Falkirk Herald*, 1868

E.P. Dennison & R. Coleman, *Historic Linlithgow*, Historic Scotland/Tuckwell Press, 2000

John Ferguson, *Ecclisia Antiqua*, Oliver & Boyd, 1905

William F. Hendrie, *Six Hundred Years a Royal Burgh*, John Donald, 1989

William Hutton, *Simon Moneypenny, or Linlithgow Marches in Olden Times*, Waldie, 1877

Bruce Jamieson, *The Reds – Linlithgow Rugby Football Club*, 1995

Eric Linklater, *Voyage of the 'Challenger'*, Cardinal, 1972

Jean Lyndsay, *The Canals of Scotland*, David & Charles, 1968

T.S. Muir, *Linlithgowshire*, Cambridge University Press, 1915

George Penney, *Linlithgowshire*, Stevenson of Edinburgh, 1831

Basil Skinner, *History of the Union Canal*, Linlithgow Union Canal Society, 1990

Alexander Smith, *Dreamthorpe*, Oxford University Press, 1863

Ronald P.A. Smith, *Linlithgow Old and New*, Linlithgow Civic Trust, 1996

T.C. Smout, *A History of the Scottish People 1560 – 1830*, Fontana Press, 1985

George Waldie, *Linlithgow*, Waldie, 1879

Chronology

1138	King David makes reference to 'a great church of Linlithgow'.
1242	St Michael's Church dedicated by Bishop David de Bernham of St Andrews.
1301	Although it is thought a Royal Manor existed in the mid 12th century, the first positive reference to royal residence is in 1301, when it is known a chamber was prepared for Edward 1 of England.
1368	Linlithgow included in the Court of the Four Burghs, given custody of the Scottish standard peck and firlot measure.
1389	Linlithgow acknowledged as a burgh.
1424	Most of the town destroyed by fire.
1513	James IV sees a warning vision in St Michael's prior to taking off for Flodden.
1535	Erection of Cross Well.
1538	Building of fountain in palace courtyard.
1539	Performance of Sir David Lyndsay's satire, *The Three Estates*.
1541	Minute of Council records the Riding of the Marches.
1542	Mary Queen of Scots born in Linlithgow palace.
1650	Cromwell stays at Linlithgow Palace while his troops damage Cross Well and an old town house.
1738	James Glen appointed Governor of South Carolina.
1745	Prince Charles Edward Stuart takes up residence in the palace.
1746	The Duke of Cumberland arrives in town. The palace is fired by his army.
1787	Burns visits the town as part of a Highland tour.
1789	Birth of Stephen Mitchell, founder of the Mitchell Library in Glasgow.
1807	Cross Well rebuilt.
1819	Work starts on the twelve-arch aqueduct over the River Avon.

1822	Opening of the Union Canal.
1840	St John's Evangelical Church completed.
1847	David Waldie gives recommendation to Sir James Simpson on the use of chloral ether.
1848	Curlers enjoy 'a Grand Match' on Linlithgow Loch.
1865	Linlithgow Bowling Club founded.
1872	Wyville Thomson of Bonsyde leads the *Challenger* expedition.
1874	Completion of St Ninian's Craigmailen Church of Scotland.
1889	Formation of Linlithgow Rose Football Club.
1889	Building of Town Hall completed.
1894	Linlithgow Academy opens its doors at the West Port.
1904	Nobels, the manufacturers of explosives, set up a factory to cater for the needs of the shale industry.
1911	Green Man statue erected to John Hope, 7th Earl of Hopetoun, first Governor General of Australia.
1913	Linlithgow Golf Club comes into being.
1914	George v holds court in the Great Hall of Linlithgow Palace.
1915	16th century doocot and gardens given to burgh in memory of Provost Alexander Learmonth.
1928	Formation of West Lothian County Cricket Club.
1928	Dedication of St Mildred's Episcopal Church.
1942	Laetare International Youth Centre founded by Father Michael McGovern.
1943	First appearance of Linlithgow Players.
1955	Her Majesty Queen Elizabeth holds reception in palace.
1956	Formation of Linlithgow Reed Band.
1957	Hamilton Lands in High Street restored by National Trust.
1964	West Lothian win the Cricket Counties Championship.
1965	Rose Football Club win the Scottish Cup.
1965	Closure of the Union Canal.
1969	Formation of Linlithgow Arts Guild.
1972	Opening of the Edinburgh–Stirling motorway with its Linlithgow bypass.

1973	The canal section between Linlithgow and Winchburgh is reopened.
1974	Beecraigs Country Park comes into being.
1975	Local Government reorganisation takes place. Court of the Deacons of the Ancient and Royal Burgh instituted with responsibility for continuing the traditions of the Marches.
1976	Formation of Linlithgow Union Canal Society.
1980	Linlithgow Scottish Country Dance Club formed.
1984	West Lothian again win County Cricket Championship.
1984	Pupil exchange takes place between Linlithgow Academy and the Paul Eduard school in Guyancourt, which leads to twinning arrangement between the two towns.
1991	Linlithgow Heritage Trust formed to take over the development and running of the town's museum at Annet House.
1999	First Folk Festival organised by the Linlithgow Folk Festival Association.
2002	Rose again win the Scottish Cup. New stand erected at Prestonfield.
2004	Linlithgow Rugby Club Choir perform in China.
2006	Twinning Association organises an International Burns Supper in Pignitz, Bavaria.

NOTES

NOTES

NOTES

Some other books published by **LUATH** PRESS

On the Trail of Robert Service

G W Lockhart

ISBN 0 946487 24 3 PBK £7.99

The story of the Scottish bank clerk who became the Bard of the Yukon, the man who captivated the imagination of generations and painlessly introduced countless numbers to the beauties of verse.

Robert Service is famed world-wide for his verse-pictures of the Klondike goldrush. As a war poet, his work outsold Owen and Sassoon, and he went on to become the world's first million-selling poet. In search of adventure and new experiences, he emigrated from Scotland to Canada in 1890 where he was caught up in the aftermath of the raging gold fever. His vivid dramatic verse brings to life the wild, larger than life characters of the gold rush Yukon, their bar-room brawls, their lust for gold, their trigger-happy gambles with life and love.

His storytelling powers have brought Robert Service enduring fame, particularly in North America and Scotland, where he is something of a cult figure. Starting in Scotland, *On the Trail of Robert Service* follows service as he wanders through British Columbia, California, Oregon, Mexico, Cuba, Russia, Turkey, and the Balkans, finally 'settling' in France.

Wallace Lockhart's relish for a well-told tale in popular verse led him to fall in love with the verse of Robert Service and write his biography. He has enjoyed the full support and co-operation of Service's family. This revised edition includes a new foreword by the poet's daughter, Iris Service Davies, plus additional photographs of scenes from the Klondike and of Robert Service from around the world.

Highland Balls and Village Halls

G W Lockhart

ISBN 0 946487 12 X PBK £6.95

A welcome return for the book acknowledged as a classic in Scottish dancing circles world-wide. Wallace Lockhart has thoroughly updated this new edition, and added chapters on Freeland Barbour, the Scottish Traditions of Dance Trust and dancing around the world.

This book is an open invitation to the growing numbers of people becoming aware of and involved in Scottish dancing to dip in a little deeper, and to those already aimmersed to dip deeper still!

Wallace Lockhart is leader of Quern and a familiar figure at music and dance events in Scotland and overseas. He is delighted to be able to contribute to the new dynamism to be found in the Scottish dance tradition by sharing his knowledge and enthusiasm.

What marked Wallace Lockhart's book out from the others, however, was the enthusiasm born of personal experience and an affection for the subject often buried by more academic commentators.

DAVID FRANCIS, Edinburgh Folk Festival

An excellent and very readable insight into the traditions and customs of Scottish country dancing.

SUNDAY POST

A delightful survey of Scottish dancing and custom. Informative, concise and opinionated.

THE HERALD

Fiddles and Folk

G W Lockhart

ISBN 0 946487 38 3 PBK £7.95

In *Fiddles and Folk*, Wallace Lockhart meets up with many of the people who have created the renaissance of Scotland's music today.

From Dougie MacLean, the Battlefield Band, the Whistle-binkies, the Scottish Fiddle Orchestra, the McCalmans and many more come the stories that break down the musical barriers between Scotland's past and present, and between the diverse musical forms which have woven together to create the dynamism of the music today.

For anyone whose heart lifts at the sound of fiddle or pipes, *Fiddles and Folk* provides a delightful journey, full of humour and respect, in the company of the performers who have taken Scotland's music around the world and come back singing.

The Scottish Wedding Book

G W Lockhart

ISBN 1 84282 010 9 PBK £12.99

Church, registry office or castle?
What should the bride wear?
How should the kilt be worn?
Who does what on the big day?
What are the important behind-the-scene arrangements?

How do we find a band and a piper?

What are the origins of handfasting?

All this and much, much more. The ideal engagement present, essential reading for all brides and grooms to be. Bridesmaids, best men and fathers of the bride might like to dip in too.

This book covers the traditions that make Scottish weddings so distinctive. It includes all the technical and legal information necessary for a church or registry office ceremony, plus useful checklists, a Scots language version of the wedding service and locations of Scottish Kirks worldwide – how to have a memorable Scottish wedding whether within or outwith Scotland. Kilts, dresses, customs, duties and dances: everything that makes a guid Scots hooley.

All in all The Scottish Wedding Book *is an in-depth guide to everything you need to know to plan your Scottish wedding, whether you're wanting a traditional or more modern day.*
PERTHSHIRE ADVERTISER

I'd call this a companion book, a learned little friend to have at your side should you be thinking of getting wed in Scotland . . . covers everything from donning the kilt to dancing the night away to the origins of the silly nonsense put about by excitable aunties. Bound to sell well given the Madonna-inspired popularity of Caledonian nupitals, and deservedly so.
THE HERALD

Blackburn: the story of West Lothian's cotton and coal town

Sybil Cavanagh

ISBN 1 905222 40 8 PBK £10.99

Sybil Cavanagh's study of the development of her adopted home charts the survival and development of a community shaken by continual economic insecurity. From the Agricultural to the Industrial Revolution; from cotton to coal; from depression to development, Blackburn's turbulent history is at once representative of the hardships facing small industrial towns in Scotland, yet peculiarly unique. A village held together by the need to work for its living, Blackburn has weathered devastating blows – from the personal disaster of fire to the national calamity of post-war depression – to become the town it is today. This is a comprehensive history of industry in Blackburn, from the building of the Cotton Mill in 1793 to the advent of British Leyland in the 1960s; it is also a study of the physical development of Blackburn, beginning with George Moncrieff moving the whole village in the 1770s and continuing to the present West Lothian Council's town-planning efforts in housing, education and recreation. Sybil Cavanagh's epic chronicle also pays tribute to the contribution of individuals to the life and character of modern Blackburn, and the sense of community spirit that endures to this day.

Hail Philpstoun's Queen... and other tales from the shale

Barbara and Marie Pattullo

ISBN 1 84282 094 X PBK £6.99

Mother and daughter team Barbara and Marie Pattullo take us back to the days of Rows houses and horse drawn grocers' vans, to summer gala days and thriving village sports clubs. Back to a life of walking to school, coping with life at war so close to the Forth and socials at the village hall.

To a time when working life may have been hard but community spirit and village pride were well-founded.

It is that spirit, and that pride, that this book aims to record, and to honour.

I warmly applaud the authors for the skill with which they have woven into a verbal tapestry information they have gleaned from a variety of sources and, above all, for their assiduity in tracking down events and relationships which would otherwise be lost for ever.

TAM DALYELL

Shale Voices

Alistair Findlay
ISBN 0 946487 63 4 PBK £10.99
ISBN 0 946487 78 2 HBK £17.99

Shale Voices offers a fascinating insight into shale mining, an industry that employed genera-tions of Scots, had an impact on the social, political and cultural history of Scotland and gave birth to today's large oil compa-nies. Author Alistair Findlay was born in the shale mining village of Winchburgh and is the fourth son of a shale miner, Bob Findlay, who became editor of the *West Lothian Courier*. *Shale Voices* combines oral history, local jour-nalism and family history. The generations of communities involved in shale mining provide, in their own words, a unique documentation of the industry and its cultural and political impact. Photographs, drawings, poetry and short stories make this a thought provoking and entertaining account. It is much a joy to dip into and feast the eyes on as to read from cover to cover.

Alistair Findlay has added a basic source material to the study of Scottish History that is invaluable and will be of great benefit to future generations. Scotland owes him a debt of gratitude for undertaking this work.

TAM DALYELL

Pumpherston: the story of a shale oil village

Sybil Cavanagh
ISBN 1 84282 015 X PBK £10.99
ISBN 1 84282 011 7 HBK £17.99

In 1884 the Pumpherston Oil Works was built and a substan-tial village came into being. The Pumpherston Oil Company is seen in the wider context of the shale oil industry. The story of its successes and failures is fol-lowed through the era of Scottish Oils and BP to the close-down of the shale oil industry in Scotland in 1962.

The village was built, supervised and patron-ised by the oil companies. A strange culture emerged in which the employers intervened in all aspects of their employees' lives, whether at work, at home or at leisure.

This fascinating book also looks at the rich social life that grew up in the village, and the wealth of characters – high achievers as well as eccentric worthies – that will stir the memories of everyone who grew up in or remembers Pumpherston in the old days.

And the story of Pumpherston comes full circle with the cleaning up of the oil works site. BP has used pioneering technology to clear the site of the pollution from more than a cen-tury of work, and to return the area to its orig-inal rural nature.

A rich mix of historical, technical and anecdotal material makes up a book that will appeal to readers not just in the local area, but to 'Pumphy' exiles all over the world and to any-one interested in the shale oil industry and Scotland's industrial heritage.

Luath Press Limited

committed to publishing well written books worth reading

LUATH PRESS takes its name from Robert Burns, whose little collie Luath (*Gael.,* swift or nimble) tripped up Jean Armour at a wedding and gave him the chance to speak to the woman who was to be his wife and the abiding love of his life. Burns called one of 'The Twa Dogs' Luath after Cuchullin's hunting dog in Ossian's Fingal. Luath Press grew up in the heart of Burns country, and now resides a few steps up the road from Burns' first lodgings in Edinburgh's Royal Mile.

Luath offers you distinctive writing with a hint of unexpected pleasures.

Most UK and US bookshops either carry our books in stock or can order them for you. To order direct from us, please send a £sterling cheque, postal order, international money order or your credit card details (number, address of cardholder and expiry date) to us at the address below. Please add post and packing as follows: UK – £1.00 per delivery address; overseas surface mail – £2.50 per delivery address; overseas airmail – £3.50 for the first book to each delivery address, plus £1.00 for each additional book by airmail to the same address. If your order is a gift, we will happily enclose your card or message at no extra charge.

Luath Press Limited
543/2 Castlehill
The Royal Mile
Edinburgh EH1 2ND
Scotland
Telephone: 0131 225 4326 (24 hours)
Fax: 0131 225 4324
email: sales@luath.co.uk
Website: www.luath.co.uk